MOSAICS

Essential Techniques
& Classic Projects

MOSAICS
Essential Techniques
& Classic Projects

Fran Soler

Sterling Publishing Co., Inc.
New York
A Sterling/Silver Book

A QUARTO BOOK

Library of Congress Cataloging-in-Publication-Data is
available upon request.

Published by Sterling Publishing Co., Inc.
387 Park Avenue South
New York, NY 10016-8810

Copyright © 1998 Quarto Inc.

Distributed in Canada by Sterling Publishing
c/o Canadian Manda Group
One Atlantic Avenue, Suite 105
Toronto, Ontario, Canada M6K 3E7

This book was designed and produced by
Quarto Publishing plc
The Old Brewery
6 Blundell Street
London N7 9BH

Senior editor Anna Watson
Text editor Leslie Viney
Art editor Sally Bond
Designer Cathy May
Photographers Bruce Mackie, Colin Bowling, Richard Gleed
Illustrator Jennie Dooge, Ian Sidaway
Picture researcher Gill Metcalf
Editorial manager Sally MacEachern
Assistant art director Penny Cobb
Art director Moira Clinch

Typeset in Great Britain by Central Southern Typesetters,
  Eastbourne
Manufactured in Singapore by Eray Scan Pte Ltd
Printed in Singapore by Star Standard Industries (Pte) Ltd

ISBN 0-8069-6305-0

Safety Notice
Mosaic making can be dangerous, and readers should follow
safety procedures, and wear protective clothing and goggles,
at all times during the preparation of tesserae and the making
and fitting of mosaics. Neither the author, copyright holders
nor publishers of this book can accept legal liability for any
damage or injury sustained as a result of making mosaics.

Contents

Chapter 2: Mosaic Projects

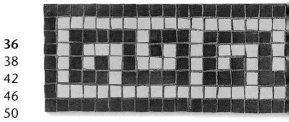

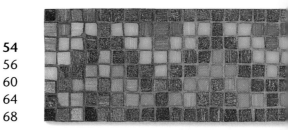

INTRODUCTION

Mosaic is a decorative art form using 'tesserae'—small pieces of glass, marble, ceramic or stone—to create images or patterns. It is an extremely adaptable medium, and endless variations of subject, material, color and application have been explored over the ages. The method of making mosaics has not changed much over the centuries and, even though it is an ancient art form, it has stood the test of time and is increasingly popular today as a versatile contemporary craft.

This sixth-century mosaic from Italy, at Sant' Apollinare Nuovo, shows how incredible detail was achieved with differing tones of natural colors.

The history of mosaics is somewhat fragmented, as they flourished during certain periods, then vanished for centuries, reappearing later on and finding favor in seemingly unconnected civilisations. The earliest mosaics were fairly basic patterns made up of pebbles, as have been discovered in Asia Minor and the gardens of ancient China. Over time smaller pebbles replaced larger ones as the patterns and images became more refined. Pebbles were set closer together to achieve better detail, some were painted to increase the range of colors, and later outlines were accentuated with lead.

Tesserae were first introduced around the fourth century B.C. These were chunks of natural stone cut into cubes, which allowed pieces to be set much closer together and so gave even greater definition to images. Early mosaics were a combination of practical decoration and artistic expression. The ancient Greeks began by using pebbles to create flooring. Aztecs used mosaic to cover ceremonial objects with precious stones. In Pompeii shrines and outdoor mosaics are thought to have been created to give the illusion of space within tiny back yards. Byzantine churches were covered in dazzling mosaics depicting religious icons, scenes from the bible and images of heaven.

As subsequent empires spread through conquest, trade or religion, demand for mosaics increased. Techniques improved as artisans travelled and passed on their skills, until eventually mosaics spread over the continents and throughout the world. Micromosaics, made from tiny close-set tesserae, became popular during the Renaissance. Although technically brilliant, they seemed to lack a certain something, being more of an alternative medium for fine artists rather than what we think of today as mosaic.

At the beginning of this century mosaics became popular once again, due to increased interest in the decorative arts. Art Nouveau used mosaics for highly decorative purposes, and this renewed interest was embraced by artists and architects alike. One of this century's most famous architects, Antoni Gaudí, took mosaics to new heights—literally—by covering buildings, park benches and even rooftops in Barcelona with a multitude of multicolored ceramic tile mosaics, leading the way for other mosaic makers to follow.

Unsurprisingly, during and for quite sometime after the two World Wars, the art of mosaic making was largely neglected.

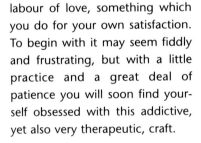

The 1950s saw a rather uninspired resurgence of architectural mosaics in all kinds of utilitarian environments. Mosaics somehow survived the vogue for covering every available wallspace with dull, lifeless swimming pool tiles unscathed, and today they are enjoying another surge of popularity, becoming an increasingly familiar sight in architectural features and public art works. Over the centuries the rules have changed, mosaics no longer need to conform to any one set of ideals—the artist has total freedom of expression and access to a wide variety of materials and colors that our predecessors could only dream of.

There is a vast wealth of both ancient and modern mosaics for you to gain inspiration from. Looking around today you will find that mosaics can be a lot more interesting than the mid-century post-war architectural cladding, 1970s shopping precincts or gloomy pedestrian subways which are still in existence. The examples and ideas shown in this book are merely the tip of the iceberg—almost anything is possible. In this book you will find many ideas and informative instructions to help you create mosaics of your own. Anyone can learn how to make a mosaic, and amazing results can be achieved using relatively simple techniques. But the secret of making a really great mosaic comes from within. Let your imagination run riot, take inspiration from things around you, use weird and wonderful bits and pieces, experiment with unusual color combinations or let the tesserae themselves inspire you. There are no quick-fix solutions in mosaic making, no short cuts and no instant solutions—it is a labour of love, something which you do for your own satisfaction. To begin with it may seem fiddly and frustrating, but with a little practice and a great deal of patience you will soon find yourself obsessed with this addictive, yet also very therapeutic, craft.

Detail of mosaic, Shah Mosque, Isfahan. Fine non-figurative details in Islamic mosaics were often made from specially cut pieces which fitted together perfectly to make extremely complex patterns.

This interior mosaic, built by the Romans at El Djem, Tunisia, shows interesting contrast between the abstract border pattern and realistic details of the thrushes.

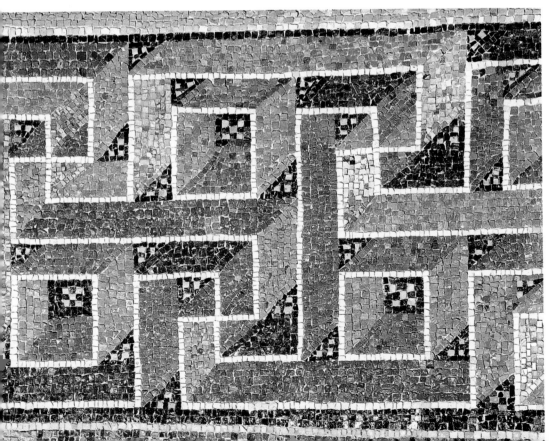

This geometric frieze is from the Mausoleum of Galla Placidia in Ravenna, Italy. With its bright colors and three-dimensional optical illusions it looks thoroughly modern, but in fact dates from the Byzantine Empire.

BEFORE YOU START

You don't need much to begin your first mosaic, just a good simple design, some old tiles and the minimum of tools. Soon you'll discover that mosaics are an addictive, absorbing and inexpensive craft, immensely enjoyable to make, and accessible to all as stunning results can be achieved by using relatively simple techniques. But beware, once you have embarked on your first mosaic you may soon be hooked!

MATERIALS AND EQUIPMENT

Tesserae

Tessera is a Roman word meaning "cube." Many tesserae are used to make a mosaic, and they come in various different materials, each with its own quality that forms an intrinsic part of the mosaic.

Smalti

These are the classic mosaic material—small, thick, rectangular chunks of handmade Italian glass. Being handmade, smalti is expensive, but comes in a vast range of colors and also possesses amazing light-reflecting qualities. The sizes vary slightly, usually approx ⅖ x ⅗in (10 x 15mm) and are of fairly uneven thickness. This makes them unsuitable for jobs where a flat surface is required, such as floors, but it is that same unevenness that catches the light and makes a mosaic sparkle. Also because of the uneven surface, smalti is not usually grouted—the idea being that when the smalti is pushed down onto the tile adhesive, it pushes the adhesive into the spaces, providing a kind of self-grouting. For a coverage of 1sq.ft. (30 x 30cm) you will need approximately 3lb (1.35kg) of smalti.

Gold and silver smalti

Extensively used by Byzantine artisans when making religious icons, these are also handmade Italian glass and have real gold and silver leaf pressed into the tile. These are available plain or smooth and also with a rippled surface. These tesserae can also be used upside down with great effect, because the gold has a shiny green underside, and the silver has a shiny blue underside. Although they are more expensive than regular smalti, even a few pieces used sparingly can add sparkle and transform an otherwise dull mosaic into a glimmering work of art.

Vitreous glass

Also made of glass, these are manufactured in regular squares. The uppermost side is smooth and flat, while the underside is rippled for adhesion. These are an ideal material for beginners, as they are thin, flat and easy to cut. They also give a flat surface and can be used for all kinds of projects. Vitreous glass tesserae come in a wide variety of colors and can be bought loose or on brown paper sheets.

Ceramic tesserae

Made from vitrified clay, these are available in a muted range of colors, usually browns, ochers, terracotta and black and white with a matte finish. They are extremely hard wearing and therefore suitable for floors, but have a tendency to stain if not properly sealed. Again, these can be bought loose or on sheets.

Ceramic tiles

The range of colors, textures and patterns of household ceramic tiles is endless. They are cheap, easy to cut and can be used with great effect. They are extremely versatile but are unsuitable for some projects, such as outdoor mosaics, as they are not necessarily frostproof. You may have some old unwanted tiles hiding in the cupboard that can be used to practice your cutting technique.

Collected objects

Broken plates, buttons, beads, bottle caps, stained glass, mirror, shell, pebbles. . . Anything that you find that can be broken up and arranged in a pattern has the potential to become part of a mosaic. Broken pottery is a great source of mosaic material, but is unlikely to be frostproof, so not suitable for outdoor use and also not hard wearing nor strong enough to be used on floors.

Surfaces

Almost any surface can be made suitable for the application of mosaic. First check that the surface is strong, dry and stable enough to take the weight of the mosaic and that the surface has been properly prepared before starting work. When working on furniture or walls, ensure that features such as drawers and doors can open correctly, and work around fixtures such as handles and light fittings.

Ceramic

Choose a thick, heavy base when putting mosaic onto ceramic. Terracotta garden pots and planters work very well, as do strong plates, bowls and vases. If applying mosaic onto a glazed surface, rub it down with coarse sandpaper and prime it so that the adhesive can grip properly.

Wood

Many of the projects in this book are on wooden bases. Medium density fiberboard or particleboard is a cheap and versatile alternative, easy to cut with a jigsaw and available in different thicknesses. These should not be used for outdoor items, however, as they will warp if they get wet. Wooden furniture or frames are also ideal surfaces. If the wood has been varnished or painted then rub it down with coarse sandpaper, and seal and prime it with a solution of white or yellow craft glue and water.

Glass

You can mosaic onto glass surfaces such as vases and bottles. Special glass glues must be used to stick the tesserae into position. Stained glass mosaic gives an interesting effect on glass, for example, in the case of candle holders where the flame flickers through the glass giving off beautiful multi-colored beams.

Metal

You can also put mosaic on to metal surfaces, such as a garden table. The surface must be roughened up with wire wool before priming, and any rust spots treated before you begin.

Cement

If in doubt as to whether or not a floor is suitable for mosaic, it is worth seeking the advice of a professional. When starting from scratch, a floor will need to be professionally skimmed and left to dry completely before beginning the mosaic application.

Glues and Adhesives

There are various kinds of glues and adhesives that are used for the different stages of making mosaics. Which glue you use depends on the size and siting of the finished piece.

White or yellow craft glue

This is a versatile glue that can be used for sticking tesserae down when using the direct method and also for sealing surfaces where the mosaic will be placed by making a solution of glue and water (1 part glue: 4 parts water). This solution is painted onto the surface and left to dry thoroughly before you begin to stick the tesserae down.

Epoxy resin

This is a two-part glue that comes in a double syringe or two tubes, one for the resin and the other for the hardener. Equal quantities of each are mixed together to create a very strong glue which can be used for working in the direct method, to stick tesserae into place, and it is suitable for both outdoor and indoor use. When working with epoxy glue, it is very important to work quickly, in a well ventilated room, as it has a fast drying time and gives off unpleasant fumes.

Wallpaper paste

This is a water-based glue used to hold tesserae onto paper when working in the "indirect" method as the tesserae are only to be held onto the paper temporarily. If working with pre-gummed brown paper, there is no need to use adhesive; simply wet the paper before sticking on the tesserae.

Grout

There are many different kinds of grout available. Some kinds are more suitable for outdoors, some are more waterproof and some set faster than others. You may want to buy pre-mixed grout, but powdered grout is very easy to use and much more economical. You can buy colored grouts, or color the grout yourself using pigments or paints. Often grout colors appear stronger when wet. Mix up a sample and allow to dry overnight for a better example of the finished result.

Cement

Cement is strong, cheap and versatile—suitable for most projects indoors and out. Its natural color is neutral but can be easily colored using cement dye. It is a good idea to experiment with the dyes before using them on the mosaic as they are very strong and permanent. When working with cement it is important to wear rubber gloves and to remember to store any unmixed cement in a plastic container somewhere dry.

Tools

Don't be put off by the number of things you will need, because many of them are everyday household objects. However, some will have to be obtained from hardware stores or specialist suppliers.

For cutting and sticking tesserae

1 glue brush
2 tile scorer
3 glass cutter
4 tile cutters
5 mosaic nippers
6 hammer and hardie (not shown, see Cutting Techniques, p.26)

For cleaning

7 cloths
8 sponge
9 scouring pads and sandpaper

For grouting

10 bowl
11 flat trowel
12 grout spreader
13 squeegee
14 palette knife
15 trowel
16 bucket (not shown)
17 plastic container (not shown)

Safety Equipment

Always wear the appropriate safety equipment when working. When cutting tesserae of any kind you must take precautions to protect yourself from accidents as splinters are extremely sharp and unpleasant and dust particles can irritate eyes and lungs.

Shoes (not shown)
Protect yourself from walking on any overlooked glass shards.

Apron
To protect your clothing.

Safety glasses
It is very important to wear these while cutting to protect eyes from splinters.

Rubber gloves
You may find that surgical gloves are better for detailed work, such as cutting and nibbling tesserae into shape.

Filter mask
To protect from breathing in dust particles.

Dustpan and brush
Sweep up any litter with the brush, as sharp shards can be dangerous.

Workspace

You may be lucky enough to have a spare room or a space in the garage to set up a workspace. Wherever you work, there are some basic requirements.

Storage
Glass jars and clear plastic bags are the most practical way to store your different tesserae. Make sure you have strong, solid shelving as jars and jars of tesserae can be very heavy. Powdered grout and cement need to be stored in lidded containers in a dry place.

Good lighting
Both in daylight and in the evening. When working on intensely detailed work it is essential to have good lighting.

Ventilation
Making mosaics can be a messy business. The dust from breaking up tesserae is often so fine that you can't see it. Also some of the adhesives and grouts give off unpleasant fumes so ventilation is very important.

Drawing desk
If space allows, it is a good idea to have another "clean" desk for drawing and designing, preferably close to a window or source of natural light.

Running water
Access to water is very important: you will need water at various stages of the work, for mixing grout and cement, and cleaning.

Workbench
A strong solid table that is at a good height for you to work at both sitting and standing.

Always wear safety equipment when working. Do not bring food or drink into your work area when you are cutting tesserae. Also try to prevent children and pets from wandering in.

Outside area
If you have access to a yard or any outdoor space, it is helpful to use when doing messy jobs such as grouting or mixing cement. You may also prefer to work outside when cleaning cemented mosaics with strong chemical cleaners, such as floor or patio cleaners.

Flooring
Ideally a durable hard floor that can be easily brushed and scrubbed. If you have carpet always put down a drop sheet before you start and vacuum the room when finished in case there are any tesserae shards.

Equipment for Designing

Again, don't be discouraged by the list of things that you will need for designing—many of these items you may already have and those which you don't can be easily obtained from an art supplier.

1 Craft knife
2 Marking pens
3 Compasses
4 Pencils
5 Sketchbook
6 Ruler
7 Graph paper
8 Tracing paper
9 Gummed brown paper

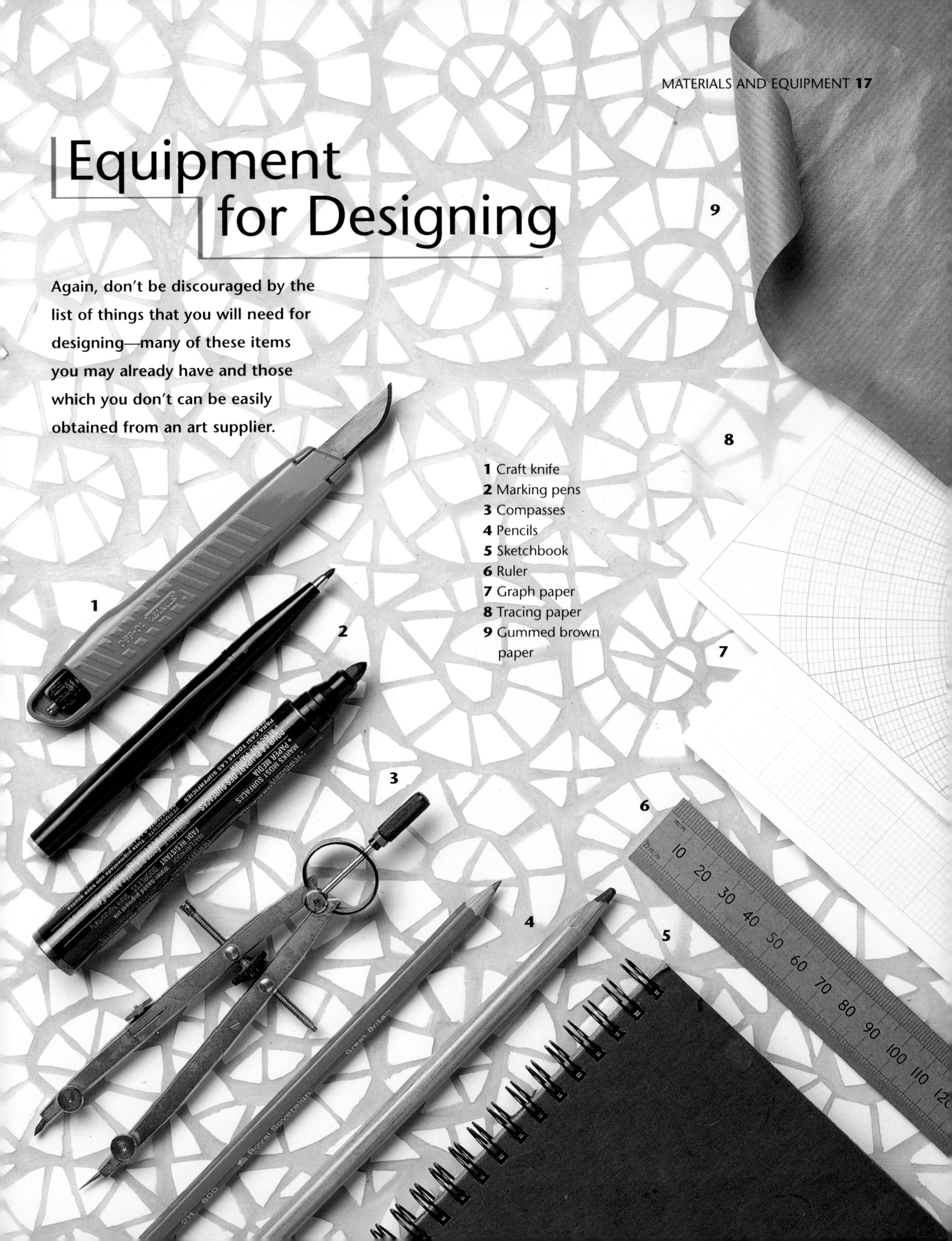

Designing your Mosaic

There are no hard and fast rules for designing a mosaic, but there are a few things to consider carefully before embarking on your first design. The most important is the idea; the image or pattern combined with the tesserae and the application and siting of the finished mosaic. Keep the ideas simple at first; perhaps work on a small object or panel for your first mosaic and resist the temptation of making something large and overambitious to start with.

This modern sculpture draws on both classical and natural forms to produce a highly original piece with a distinctly marine feeling.

Techniques and skills are things that you can only learn and master fully with experience, so attempting a large, complicated project could quickly lead to frustration and loss of interest. Mosaic making requires a lot of concentration and a great deal of patience; mistakes are inevitable at the early stages, but with perseverance and plenty of time allowed for practice, you can achieve amazing results.

You must first think about the finished mosaic, where it is going to be placed and whether it would be suitable for that particular environment. A large mosaic in a very small room may be a little overpowering—a certain amount of distance between the mosaic and the viewer is necessary, so that the viewer can see the mosaic as a whole and not just individual tesserae. The design should also consider the form of the object or surface where the mosaic will be done. For example, in order to fit around a curved object, such as a vase or pot, a pattern may need to be modified slightly, or details may require more, or less, spacing out. Or the design may be too complicated to fit around a narrow picture frame, in which case the design could be simplified further. Cramming too many patterns into a small space is not necessarily the most effective way to achieve a design, but rather taking elements of the pattern and expanding them to fit the shape is much easier and even more striking. Any design can be modified and adjusted to suit whatever kind of application you require, and some designs will simply work better on particular items.

When you are designing a project, such as a new bathroom, try to resist the temptation of giving into fashion, and designing in this season's colors, or you may find that by the time your dream bathroom is complete, fashion has moved on. Also consider the cost, both in materials and time. If making the floor completely from mosaic is out of the question, then think about making a doorstep or a paving stone. Similarly, if you cannot put mosaic on your walls, work onto a panel instead. Objects such as boxes, tables and frames need to be strong enough to take the weight of the tesserae. This is even more important in the case of floors and walls, particularly if you are working with a very heavy material such as marble. If you are in any doubt about the strength and suitability of a wall or floor, it is worth seeking the advice of a professional builder before starting.

Before investing in expensive materials, take a look at things you already have that can be broken up and used as tesserae, such as any unwanted bathroom tiles or pieces of broken pottery or china—these are the type of tesserae to incorporate into your first mosaic. Use these to practice cutting techniques, and to get to know your tools and how to use them. At first cutting tesserae can be extremely frustrating, but by following the guidelines and persevering you will get the hang of it and find a way of working that suits you.

The different types of tesserae each have their own qualities, with some more suitable for certain projects than others, both aesthetically and practically. Smalti has extraordinary light-reflecting properties and comes in an enormous variety of rich and vibrant colors, and gold and silver smalti, although expensive, can be used sparingly to add a bit of sparkle to an otherwise flat mosaic. Since it is made of glass, smalti is not suitable for use on floor mosaics. Vitreous glass tesserae are smooth, flat and strong. Widely used for swimming pools and architectural mosaics, these tesserae are practical and durable enough to withstand any application. Using ceramic tiles is a great way of covering large surfaces, as they are easy to work with and are available in every imaginable color. However, not all ceramic tiles are frostproof, so it is worth checking the manufacturer's label if you are working on an outdoor project. Choose the tesserae to suit both the environment and the mosaic itself, and think about the type of grouting that will both complement the tesserae and enhance the mosaic.

Old bathroom tiles are ideal to use for practicing cutting techniques.

Simplicity is the key to a successful mosaic design: remember that you are creating a mosaic image rather than a painting or illustration and concentrating on tiny details will inevitably lead to frustration and probable disappointment. Inspiration can be drawn from almost anywhere, so look around at your environment for ideas; refer to books, look at textiles and ceramics, visit galleries, parks, zoos, historic buildings, museums and churches. Rather than going for an exact copy of something that you admire, take the essence of that idea and incorporate it into your own unique design. You don't have to be a fantastic artist or draftsman to design a mosaic, just put your idea down onto paper. From that initial sketch, make

Inspiration for a design can come from almost anywhere. Make sketches of objects to get a feel for the shapes and develop ones which you find interesting.

Make lots of sketches, try out different compositions and play around with color before rushing into the mosaic.

another drawing, but this time eliminate any unnecessary details and stylize the design using bold clear shapes. When you are happy with the design, draw it out again onto a sheet of graph paper, this time to the exact size and shape you require. Look carefully at your design and think about the composition, the spacing between motifs or patterns, and the balance between background and foreground; something that is much easier to do once the design has been drawn out in full size. Take the tesserae that you will be using and lay them loosely on top of the design, which will give you a fairly good idea of what the mosaic will look like, and play around with the tesserae until you are happy. With time and practice the elements of what makes a good design and what suits your own creative style will become apparent, but to start with simply concentrate on the actual process of putting together a mosaic— and enjoy yourself.

Stunning results can be achieved by allowing plenty of time for designing and planning.

Opus

The way in which the individual pieces of tesserae are cut and arranged dictates the overall rhythm and movement of the mosaic. Each piece laid down partly determines the position of the next, gradually building up a mosaic that fits together beautifully and flows smoothly. There are several different techniques of laying the tesserae, each with its own qualities, and these are known as "opus."

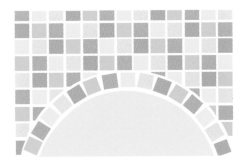

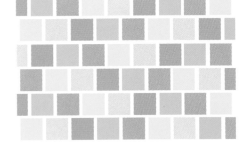

Andamento

The word used to describe the flow or direction of the mosaic, determined by the placement of the tesserae and the grout lines.

Opus Regulatum

A technique used originally by the Romans, where tesserae of the same shape are arranged in straight horizontal lines (but not lining up vertically), giving a similar effect to the pattern of a brick wall.

Opus Tesellatum

Square tesserae are arranged in horizontal and vertical lines to form a grid-like pattern. This is an effective technique for filling in backgrounds.

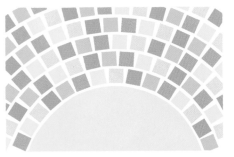

Opus Musivum

This technique is a continuation of *opus vermiculatum*, where the tesserae continue to flow outward following the contours of the outline, filling the entire background. This gives a great sense of movement and rhythm, and really brings a mosaic to life.

Opus Vermiculatum

Square tesserae are used to outline the main design or foreground details, closely following the contours of the shape and emphasising the outline in a smooth, flowing, worm-like fashion (*vermis* is the Latin word for worm). This technique creates a halo effect around the main design.

Interstices

These are the spaces in between the tesserae. Interstices play a very important part in the make up of the mosaic and the overall feeling of the work. The texture and color of grout or cement used to fill the interstices can change the effect of the mosaic very dramatically and this is something that should be considered carefully when planning the design for a mosaic. Looking closely at Roman mosaics and how the tesserae were laid can be both informative and inspiring.

Choosing Your Colors

The color wheel is often used to explain how colors relate to and interact with each other throughout the spectrum. A basic six-color wheel shows the two basic types of color: primary and secondary.

RED

ORANGE

PURPLE

YELLOW

BLUE

GREEN

Primary colors are red, yellow and blue. Positioned at equal distances apart on the wheel, these are pure colors and cannot be mixed from any other colors.

Secondary colors are orange, green and purple. These are positioned in between the primaries on the color wheel and are made up of a mixture of the two primary colors on either side.

Complementary colors are positioned directly opposite each other on the color wheel: red / green, yellow / purple, blue / orange. The complementary color of a primary is made up of a mixture of the other two primary colors; green contains no red, purple has no yellow, and orange no blue.

Contrasting colors

Maximum contrast between two colors can be obtained by the juxtaposition of a primary and its complementary color. This intensifies and mutually enhances the two colors. Complementary colors that are of equal intensity and brilliance create an optical effect, making the colors appear to flicker against each other. This is important to consider when choosing tesserae for a mosaic, as this flickering and flashing effect will distract from the mosaic itself and confuse the eye. Good contrast can be achieved simply by changing the surrounding or background color of the design; colors appear darker when surrounded by a light background and lighter when against a dark background.

The red tile here will appear darker when surrounded by a paler color

The same red tile will appear brighter when surrounded by a darker color

Pale grey surrounding a dark charcoal motif

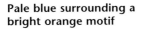

Pale blue surrounding a bright orange motif

Shades and tones

Strong outlines around details or motifs can be created by placing two different tones of the same color next to one another. Again, this enhances both colors, making the light one appear lighter and the dark one relatively darker, for example, with a pale gray background around a dark charcoal motif. Alternatively, another way of creating strong outline contrast is to use lighter shades of complementary colors, for example, using a pale blue background around a bright orange motif or pale green around bright red.

Warm and cool colors

A sense of space and distance between background and foreground can be achieved by the use of pale, dusty colors (such as pale blues, creams, beiges and soft purples) in the background and strong, clean colors in the foreground. Colors such as red, orange and yellow have a natural tendency to jump forward whereas blues and greens tend to recede. Groups of colors possess different "temperatures." Colors such as reddish purples, pinks, reds, oranges, yellows and light greens are all warm colors. Cool colors are turquoise greens, mid greens, dark green, blues, ultramarine and bluey purples. These color groups form the two opposite halves of the color spectrum.

Warm colors

Cool colors

Mixing colors of tesserae

Different colors of tesserae can be combined to give an overall effect of another color. For example, using a combination of pale blue, cobalt, turquoise, cyan, midnight blue and a little purple will give the overall appearance of a bright blue when viewed from a distance. By varying the amounts of the different colors combined, the overall color can be changed considerably. If the mosaic is too bright, the color can be toned down by the addition of a few softer-toned tesserae of the same basic color, spread evenly throughout the area. In the same way, an area that is too dull can be brightened up by the addition of a few carefully placed brighter tesserae. This method is also a great way of introducing a little texture to an otherwise flat background. Experiment with different color groups: try mixing various shades of color, and combining different types of tesserae. The addition of a few pieces of smalti or stained glass will give sparkle, and adding some unglazed ceramic tesserae or pebbles can add subtlety.

This mixture of yellows and blues gives an over all impression of green.

Brighten up your mosaic by adding strongly colored smalti or gold smalti

A pale grout appears to lighten the colors of the mosaic.

Darker grout with the same color tesserae produces an entirely different result.

Colored grout

Simply changing the color of the grout will dramatically affect the overall feeling of the mosaic. Since the grout itself and the spaces in between the tesserae play such an important role in the mosaic, it is important to consider the grouting while thinking about the design. White grout can be very harsh, particularly when used to fill a mosaic of dark or bright colors. The bright white tends to draw the eye to the gaps rather than the colors, but works very well for pale mosaics, including work with mirror tesserae. Dark grouts enhance the color of the tesserae. It is very effective for highly colored mosaics, but can dominate pale colors. Experiment with small batches of grout, try coloring grout with dyes, pigments or paints to achieve maximum contrast or subtle variations.

Available color ranges

Shown below are examples of smalti and vitreous glass which are available from specialist suppliers in a variety of colors, shapes and finishes. These are sometimes sold by weight in mixed bags with a random assortment of colors. This a good idea if you're just starting out as you will have a selection of many different colors—maybe only a few of each—but enough to get you started.

Vitreous glass tesserae

Smalti

Gold and silver smalti

Gold-veined vitreous glass tesserae

Basic Techniques

Cutting Techniques

Cutting tesserae is the technique that requires the most practice and patience. At first it can seem hopeless, and mistakes are inevitable, but it is amazing how quickly your cutting skills will improve. It is a good idea to practice by cutting any old unwanted ceramic tiles that you may already have.

Equipment
tile scribe / scorer
tile cutters
mosaic nippers
steel ruler
mask and safety glasses

Hammer and hardie

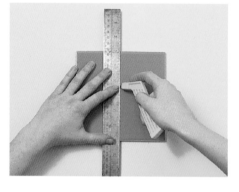

1 Score a line along the center of the tile by applying pressure with the tile scribe. Be careful not to let the scribe slip across the tile—it helps to use a steel ruler as a guide.

2 Place the tile cutters at the edge of the tile, with the center of the tile cutter mouth lined up with the scored line. Squeeze the handles of the tile cutters slowly and firmly together, and the tile will break along the line.

3 Cut the tile into smaller strips by repeating the scoring and breaking process with the tile cutters. Using the mosaic nippers, break the tile strips into the desired shape by holding the nippers at the edge of the tile at the angle you require and firmly squeezing the handles together.

Hammer and hardie
These are the traditional tools used for cutting marble and smalti. Each tessera is held over the blade of the hardie and tapped firmly with the hammer, breaking it along the desired line. Allow yourself plenty of time for practice, as this is a tricky cutting technique. You must be especially careful of flying splinters.

Cutting Shapes

CUTTING SQUARES

1 First break the square tile into four equal strips.

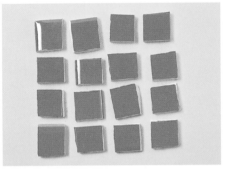

2 Divide the strips into square sections with the tile scribe and break up using the mosaic nippers.

CUTTING TRIANGLES

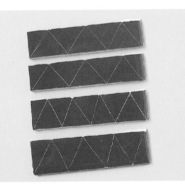

1 Break the tile into four strips and score diagonal lines in a zigzag.

2 Carefully line up the scored line with the mouth of the mosaic nippers and break into triangles.

CUTTING CURVES

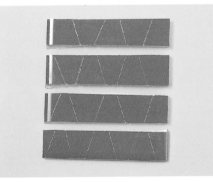

1 Score lines along the strips in alternate angled directions and cut with the mosaic nippers.

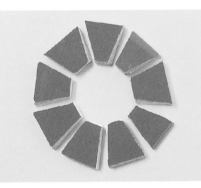

2 Create curves by playing around with the tesserae, turning them around in different directions and experimenting by placing different sides together.

Direct Mosaic-laying Method

The direct method is ideal for making your first mosaic, as the tesserae are laid the "right" way up so that the top of the tesserae become the surface of the final mosaic. You can clearly see the design progressing with every piece laid down. Think of a very simple design for your first mosaic. Limit the colors used and allow yourself plenty of time to practice cutting the tesserae and spacing the pieces together.

Materials
tracing paper
pencil
square wooden board
tiles or tesserae
white or yellow craft glue
water
acrylic paint
grout

Equipment
paintbrush
tile cutters
mosaic nippers
palette knife or mini trowel
mask and safety glasses
squeegee
sponge
lint-free cloth

1 Prepare the surface of the wood by applying a solution of craft glue and water (1 part glue: 4 parts water) with a paintbrush. Allow to dry thoroughly.

2 Enlarge the design to the size required and trace onto tracing paper. Transfer the design onto the wood with a pencil, making sure the outline is clear and defined.

3 Break up the tesserae into approximate sizes; these can be nibbled into exact shape as they are needed. Starting with the outside edge, cut the tesserae into square shapes using the mosaic nippers.

4 Closely following the design, stick the tesserae firmly onto the wood by applying a small dab of craft glue onto the bottom of the tesserae with a paintbrush, leaving a small $\frac{1}{8}$–$\frac{1}{10}$ in (2–3 mm) space between each piece.

5 To make an oval shape for the center of the star, use the mosaic nippers to nibble away at the corners of a square until it is smooth and round.

6 When all the tesserae are in place, allow the mosaic to dry thoroughly—overnight is ideal.

7 Mix a solution of water and colored acrylic paint in a bowl. Following the manufacturer's instructions, mix the colored water and the powdered grout together in a bucket, to a smooth buttery consistency.

8 Spread the grout over the mosaic with a palette knife or a mini trowel, pushing it down well into the spaces.

9 Wipe away lumps of excess grout with a rubber squeegee, making sure to smooth away any rough edges along the sides.

10 Take a damp sponge and wipe the mosaic to take off any left-over surface grout. Let it dry for 20–30 minutes before the next stage.

11 When the grout is dry to the touch, clean off the fine layer of surface grout by polishing with a dry lint-free cloth.

Indirect Mosaic- laying Method

The indirect method is a bit like working in reverse. The tesserae are stuck face down onto gummed paper, which is then set into a bed of grout and the paper washed away later when the mosaic has set. When working on a large indirect project, the design will need to be broken up into sections. When all the sections are drawn up, carefully turn the paper over and draw a mark across each of the joins—something simple that will be easy to line up later on—and also number the sections in a logical order. This should help to avoid the nightmare of putting the sections in the wrong place.

Materials
tracing paper
pencil
marking pen
gummed paper (or strong brown paper and wallpaper paste)
tiles or tesserae
grout
water

Equipment
tile cutters
mosaic nippers
trowel
mask and safety glasses
bucket
squeegee
sponge
abrasive scouring pad
lint-free cloth

1 Draw out the design to the actual size and clearly mark in the colors to be used. Play around with the tesserae on the paper to get a feel of what it will look like when completed.

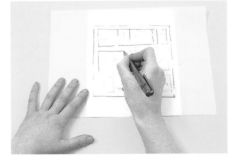

2 Trace the design onto a sheet of tracing paper with a black marking pen. Do not turn the tracing paper over yet—rub over the marking pen lines with a soft lead pencil.

3 Turn the tracing paper over and transfer the design onto the gummed paper (gummy side up) by tracing over the black marking pen lines, using a hard lead pencil. The design will now be in reverse.

4 Carefully stick the tesserae face down onto the gummed paper by wetting the surface of the piece with a wet paintbrush. If you are using ordinary brown paper fix the tesserae with a weak solution of wallpaper paste.

5 Work with one color of tesserae at a time and take extra care to follow the correct colors of the design. This is particularly tricky when working with ceramic tiles as they all look similar from the back.

6 Mix up the grout in a bucket, slowly adding water to the powder until it reaches a sloppy, melted butter consistency.

7 Make sure that the surface for the mosaic has been prepared and is dust-free. Apply a generous layer of grout to the surface with a trowel.

8 Turn the mosaic over, so the brown paper is facing toward you and place the mosaic into the space, making sure to line the edge of the mosaic with the edges of the surrounding tiles.

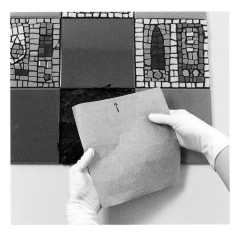

9 Smooth the mosaic down into place using a squeegee. Press down hard so that the grout moves into the spaces between the tesserae. Allow to set.

10 When the grout has set, moisten the brown paper with a wet sponge and peel off. Remove any stubborn paper and grout with a scouring pad. Check the grouting in case there are any gaps. If so, fill them in with grout and wipe any excess off with a sponge. Finally, when all the grout is dry, polish with a dry lint-free cloth.

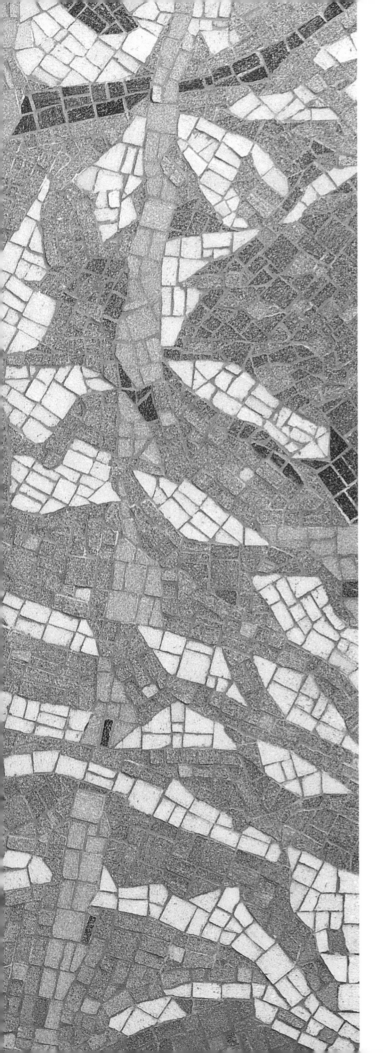

MOSAIC PROJECTS

The twenty projects in the following chapter show imaginative and inspiring examples of the wide range of methods, styles and applications used by modern mosaic makers. Each of the projects is accompanied by templates, ideas for alternative color options, clear instructions and helpful tips. Of course, there is no need to follow the templates exactly, you can add ideas of your own—choose your favorite colors, experiment with different materials, and adapt the designs to fit your own requirements. The possibilities are endless.

The earliest mosaics discovered date back to around the third millennium B.C., found near the river Tigris in Mesopotamia. These simple mosaics consisted of terracotta cones embedded into walls, their surfaces painted with bright colors. In Gordium, Asia Minor, early mosaic floors, made of pebbles arranged in simple geometric forms and set in mortar date back to the eighth century B.C. Around the fourth century B.C., Hellenic artists introduced the use of small cut cubes of stone—the first "tesserae"—and radically transformed the art of mosaic making.

CLASSICAL INSPIRATIONS

This newer method was adopted by the Romans who took to mosaic making with much enthusiasm.

With the expansion of the Roman Empire, the demand for mosaic floors grew and the use of mosaic became increasingly popular, spreading over a vast region. Examples of Roman mosaics of a wide variety of styles and subjects still survive: scenes depicting everyday life, studies of animals and birds and abstract border patterns. By the third century A.D., mosaics depicting sacred images became popular, along with the introduction of the use of glass and gold tesserae—a technique which was later used to great effect by the early Christians.

The Byzantine era, which lasted for over a thousand years, from the fifth to the fifteenth century, saw great advance-ment in skills and the development of mosaics into a highly specialized art form. Glass tesserae (smalti) became increasingly popular and eventually became the definitive material for Byzantine mosaics. Bright jewel-like colored smalti were set in mortar at slight angles to exploit the light reflective properties, and gold smalti was used to depict light emanating from sacred figures. Mosaic art was greatly patronized by the Christian church—in Ravenna in Italy many superb examples have survived, despite extensive rebuilding and restoration. In the Mausoleum of Galla Placidia (A.D. 430–50) a richly decorated cross-shaped church, the center of the vault has a cross in the middle, a deep blue background with dazzling gold stars, four symbols of evangelists at each corner and scrolling vines surrounding.

This beautifully preserved Roman floor mosaic, at El Djem in Tunisia, depicts the nine muses and their attributes, in incredible detail.

This sixth-century mosaic in the dome of the Baptistery of the Orthodox, Ravenna, uses brilliant colors and glittering gold smalti to illustrate the baptism of Christ.

An apse mosaic at Albegna, Italy, uses a night-sky blue background to set off the white motifs of stars and doves.

Sant' Apollinare Nouvo was built by the Gothic king Theodoric next to his palace around A.D. 500. The apse has since been destroyed, but the upper parts of the church walls remaining are entirely covered with mosaics depicting twenty six scenes from the life of Christ. Other important churches in Ravenna include San Vitale (which houses extraordinary mosaics depicting Christ with the Apostles and the well known mosaic of Emperor Justinian and Empress Theodora and their court) and Sant' Apollinare in Classe (at Classis, just to the southeast of Ravenna). At the Hagia Sophia, in Constantinople, the mosaic of "Christ enthroned," which depicts Emperor Constantine IX and his wife Zoe (A.D. 1042–55), has been extensively altered. Zoe had married Constantine in 1042, and his name and face replaced that of a previous husband. The portrait of Zoe, who was sixty four when she re-married, was replaced by a younger, more beautiful image. With the fall of the Byzantine Empire in the middle of the fifteenth century came a decline in the popularity of mosaics. During the Renaissance, particularly in Italy where smalti was by then being produced in Murano, there was a renewed interest in mosaics. Stylized shapes and the use of gold were rejected in favor of pictorial realism, so much so that the mosaic lost some of its true qualities and became merely a replica of paintings. Today much can be learned from looking at ancient mosaics and inspiration drawn from the vast scope of styles and techniques.

This intricate mosaic of the Three Kings is situated on the north wall of the nave at Sant' Apollinare Nuovo, in Ravenna.

Themes

religion, Christ, saints, angels

Motifs

stars, crosses, vines, animals, scrolls, doves

Materials

pebbles, stone, glass, smalti, gold

Objects

panels, walls, columns, floors

Places

RAVENNA
San Vitale, Mausoleum of Galla Placidia, Sant' Apollinare Nouvo

ISTANBUL
Hagia Sophia

VENICE
St Mark's Cathedral

SICILY
Monreal Cathedral, Church of Palermo

KIEV
Church of Hagia Sophia

This beautiful design, inspired by traditional geometric patterns and natural forms of leaves and flowers, uses cool marble tesserae in contrasting colors to create a stunning floor design that can be adapted in shape and size to transform even the most unassuming bathroom.

Geometric Marble Floor

Materials
marble
graph paper
tracing paper
strong brown wrapping paper
pencil
cement based fixative
grout
wallpaper paste

Equipment
mask and safety glasses
hammer and hardie
paintbrush
scissors
notched trowel
flat trowel
squeegee
sponge

Before you start
Working on a project of this scale and level of difficulty requires a great deal of planning, consideration and a certain amount of experience. The floor must be properly sealed and prepared in advance, and it must be strong and secure enough to take the weight of the marble—it is worth seeking professional advice from a builder or flooring expert before you start planning. Installing the mosaic is a complicated and difficult task and you will need the help of at least one other person, so again it is well worth employing a professional tiler or builder with experience in this type of work.

Draw your design onto graph paper
Measure out the floor space and work out your design on a large sheet of graph paper. As this is a repeating pattern it can easily be modified to fit the shape of your floor, either by extending or condensing the design depending on the requirements. You might find it useful to enlarge the design on a photocopier and trace the pattern onto the graph paper.

Transfer the design onto backing paper
Trace and transfer the design onto backing paper, the shiny side of strong brown wrapping paper. Mark the colors of the design into the appropriate places. Remember that you are working indirectly, so the outlines on the backing paper are the reverse of the original drawing.

Divide the pattern into sections
Turn the backing paper over and scribble boldly onto the back—this will help line the mosaic into exact position when installing. Cut the paper into sections and mark each of these clearly with a number and arrows at each edge showing which direction they face. Draw out a map of the sections, with each one numbered, so that you have a reference in case of confusion.

TIP Divide the design into sections of a manageable size for installation, by marking with a pencil and using a steel ruler for a straight edge. At the sides of each of the sections clearly mark the number and draw an arrow to denote which way up the section is to be installed. Do not cut into sections until all of the edges have been numbered and you have marked on the reverse side (see Tip on p.47).

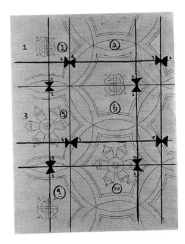

Susan Goldblatt

Template

Key

■ Dark green

■ Dark brown

■ Ocher

■ Charcoal

■ Brown

■ Pale pink

■ Light brown

■ White

Stick tesserae to backing paper

Cut the marble into manageable pieces and then into the exact shape and size with a hammer and hardie. Stick the tesserae to the backing paper with a strong solution of wallpaper paste, remembering that the surface stuck to the paper will become the surface of the final mosaic. Use the wallpaper paste sparingly so that it does not seep through the backing paper and stick to your work surface.

Line sections up evenly

Line adjacent sections up to one another when sticking tesserae to the edge of a section, so there are no unnaturally large spaces between them and the spacing of the tesserae remains constant throughout.

Install the mosaic

Lay the sections out in order next to the floor space and check the measurements one more time. In order to install the mosaic you will need to find an assistant—this is where your professional helper comes in. Work backwards from the far side of the room so that you do not find yourself wedged into a corner unable to escape for days while the cement dries! Apply cement fixative to the area of the first section and comb with a notched trowel. Place the mosaic section into position, the backing paper facing towards you, and smooth into place with a flat trowel. Repeat the process again for the next section, using the arrows to guide into position and lining up the scribble lines for the precise location.

Allow floor to dry

When all the sections are in place, leave them for four to five days for the cement to set. Then wet the backing paper with a sponge and peel the paper off at a close angle. Clean the surface with the sponge, gently rubbing away any remaining pieces of backing paper until they come loose.

Grout the mosaic

Fill in the spaces with a fine gray floor grout, being careful to work the grout carefully into the spaces. Any stubborn grout can be removed with a scrubbing brush and specialist marble cleaner.

Color Options

Marble is available in a wonderful variety of cool, subtle colors and finishes. Choose contrasting colors to give extra definition within this composition, and try adding texture by integrating a little veined marble into the details.

	Sage green
	Brown
	Ocher
	White

A subtle variation of the original, this version uses warm, natural colors to give an autumnal feel.

	Sage green
	Pale pink
	Ocher
	White
	Charcoal

Strong contrasts between the bold outlines and the pastel background result in a more contemporary look.

Roman Swirl Mirror Frame

The swirly design around this frame is a classic Roman pattern, often used for decorative borders on floors. The pattern is the same whichever way you look at it—with both colors following the same path. Many examples of this kind of repeated pattern were found in Roman art and these are known as "key patterns."

Examples of interlocking key patterns, in which two colors follow the same shape.

Materials
tracing paper
wood (or ready made wooden frame)
ceramic tiles
white or yellow craft glue
tile adhesive
grout
mirror
pencil and marking pen

Equipment
jigsaw
mask and safety glasses
tile cutters
mosaic nippers
palette knife
bucket
squeegee
sponge and dry cloth
paintbrush

Fran Soler

Prepare your surface
Begin by preparing the surface of the mirror frame. Mix a solution of craft glue and water (1 part glue: 4 parts water) and apply with a paintbrush. The frame used in this project was already made, but a simple frame can be made by cutting a circular shape from a wooden board, and cutting a smaller circle from the center using a jigsaw. The mirror can later be held into place on the back of the board, by positioning tacks around the circular cutaway and bending them firmly over the mirror.

Plan your design
Trace the design onto the wooden frame. You may have to modify the swirls to fit your frame; this can be done with the help of a compass. Mark the outlines clearly with a hard lead pencil or marking pen.

Prepare your tiles
Break up the ceramic tiles into pieces, without worrying too much about accuracy at this stage as the tesserae will need to be nibbled into specific shapes. Choose two colors to work with which complement each other and keep the colors in separate piles as you work.

Glue the tesserae in place
Apply tile adhesive to the wooden frame using a palette knife, working in small sections to avoid the adhesive drying out and becoming lumpy. Stick the tesserae into place—starting with the outside edge—working with one color at a time and nibbling the tesserae into shape as you go along. (See Cutting Shapes, p.27, for how to cut curves.) When all the tesserae have been secured in place, allow the project to dry overnight.

Grout the mosaic
In a bucket, mix up a dark gray colored grout. This can be done with a pre-colored grout or color the grout yourself by adding a dark stain or some acrylic paint to the water before adding it to the powdered

Template

Key

☐ **White ceramic**

■ **Black ceramic**

grout. Apply the grout using a palette knife, spreading generously over the mosaic and pushing down in between the spaces. Wipe off the excess with a squeegee and smooth out the edges of the frame.

Finish off the mirror

Clean off any other leftover lumps of grout with a damp sponge and let sit until the mosaic surface is dry to the touch, then polish with a dry cloth. Finally, secure the round mirror into the frame—it is best to have the mirror professionally cut to size—and then hang it in place.

TIP If the template does not fit your mirror frame, divide the frame into equal sections and draw circles in each section using a compass. Use these circles to guide you as you draw the swirls freehand, trying to make them as even in thickness as possible, but don't worry too much if they are not all exactly identical. Draw the swirls with a pencil until you are happy with the design before defining the outline with a marking pen.

Color Options

Update this traditional design with bright, contemporary colors and a combination of different textured tesserae and materials. You could also experiment with colored grout to enhance the pattern and enliven the colors.

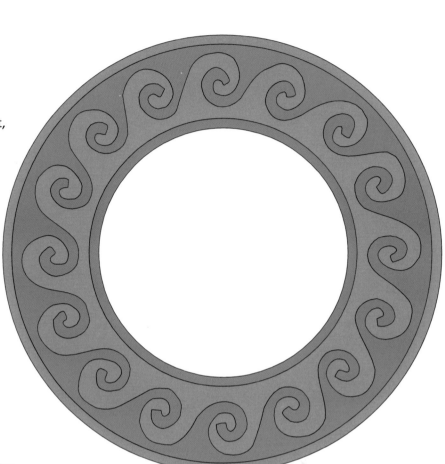

- Terracotta unglazed ceramic
- Turquoise glazed ceramic

For a striking result choose two complementary colors, such as blue and orange, and create further variation by using shiny ceramic next to unglazed tiles.

- Pale gray unglazed ceramic
- Violet unglazed ceramic

A more subtle, but equally effective result can be achieved using two pale colours of similar intensity and tone in a smooth, matte finish.

It would be unfair to suggest that this project is an easy one; it is fairly complicated and requires a great deal of planning, preparation and a certain amount of experience. Perhaps the first thing to consider before starting is the difficulty of actually installing a mosaic onto a ceiling. You will need to work with at least one other person, and preferably someone who has some experience with ceilings. It might be worth employing a professional tiler or mosaicist to help with the installation.

Marble Ceiling

Materials
marble
tracing paper
pencil
strong brown wrapping paper
flour and water
cement adhesive
grout
fine sand

Equipment
mask and safety glasses
scissors
hammer and hardie
two buckets
flat trowel
¼in (6mm) square-notched trowel
sponge

Vanessa Benson

Before you begin
The ceiling will need to be prepared with a fine layer of sand and cement at least three weeks before installing the mosaic, and any dropped ceiling must be strong enough to carry the weight of the marble mosaic. If a dropped ceiling is to be made especially for this purpose, it is worth investigating the possibility of making the mosaic directly onto the dropped ceiling before it goes up.

Prepare the design
Sketch the design to the desired shape and size, leaving ¼in (5mm) all around in case it expands during the making. This design requires mathematical calculations to make sure there is equal spacing between the wave-like shapes of the border, and the number of waves should be divisible by the number of different colors used.

Trace the design
Trace the design onto backing paper (the shiny side of strong brown wrapping paper) remembering that the installed mosaic will be a mirror image in design and shape, so the design will need to be reversed. Write the colors of the wave-like shapes onto them for reference. Turn the backing paper over and scribble boldly onto the back—like doing a puzzle, this pattern will aid the correct positioning of the sections onto the ceiling.

TIP Before cutting the backing paper into sections, turn the paper over and draw straight lines that correspond exactly with the section lines on the other side. Loosely scribble over the paper with a distinctive wobbly line—ignore the grid lines, just draw through them. The idea is to have another pattern to help align the sections when installing the mosaic.

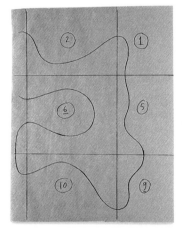

Cut the border into sections
The entire backing sheet needs to be cut into manageable sections—so that you will be able to comfortably lift it up to the ceiling with two hands. With this design, cut the border into sections and carefully divide the center into equal sections. It is very important to draw the sections first so that when it comes to sticking the tesserae into position there are no unwanted spaces and the sections cannot be detected once the mosaic is in place. Each section needs to be clearly marked with a number—attach a little piece of paper to the edge of the section on both sides so that it sticks out slightly and is always visible. It is a good

idea to draw a "map" of the mosaic with each section clearly marked and numbered on it. Do another, reversed version so that you have one for the mosaic and one for the ceiling.

Cut the marble

Cut the marble to the required shape using a hammer and hardie. Use an even thickness of marble throughout the mosaic—¼in (5mm) is ideal. Make a glue by mixing flour and water together to a milky consistency and stir on the heat until thickened. Use this glue to stick the marble tesserae to the backing paper, keeping in mind that the surface you are sticking down to the paper is the surface that will make up the visible mosaic. When sticking tesserae to the edge of a section, make sure the adjacent section is exactly in position, as if the paper had not even been cut. This guarantees the same spacing as in other parts of the mosaic, avoiding any evidence of the sections in the final result.

Mark sections on the ceiling

In order to affix the mosaic to the ceiling you will need the assistance of at least one other person, and this is where your professional helper comes in. Lay the mosaic out on a flat surface, with all the sections in position and check the measurements. Using a chalk line, draw the sections on the ceiling. Always wear safety glasses while working on ceilings at every stage of the installation.

Prepare cement and grout

While one person is mixing up a quick drying cement, the second can be mixing up the grout. Spread the cement adhesive over the area of the ceiling to take the first section. Comb the cement with a ¼in (5mm) square-notched trowel, making a thin, even bed. Meanwhile, sprinkle the first section of mosaic with a small amount of sifted dry sand—this will prevent the grout from flowing beneath the tesserae, and help to keep them clean. Spread the grout over the mosaic section, pushing it down into the crevices with a trowel.

Template

Key

Off white		Charcoal	
Sea green		Black	
White		Mid gray	
Stone		Dark brown	
Cream		Brown	
		Pumpkin	

Place mosaic sections on ceiling

Lift the mosaic section toward the ceiling and push into place with a flat trowel. Use a sponge to gently push the section into its exact position before the cement gets too hard. Wet the paper with a sponge and move onto the next section, where the same process is repeated. Line up the next section using the scribble to guide into position and press into place by tapping gently on the back with a sponge. Make sure there are no spaces between the sections of paper and that the lines of the scribble meet up exactly. Wet this second piece of paper with the sponge as you proceed to the next section and continue wetting previous sections as you work on the following ones. Do not allow any of the cement adhesive to dry on the ceiling before the sections have been placed on; apply it one section at a time, only as and when it is needed.

Repair or replace tesserae

As soon as the paper is able to be removed, pull each piece off. If any tesserae fall out, stick them back in with a little cement adhesive. If any spaces look too big, you can remove a few tesserae and replace them with larger pieces of marble—before the grout and cement sets too hard.

Clean the mosaic

Clean the mosaic when all sections have been fixed and all the paper has been removed. Quick drying cement allows almost immediate cleaning (2 hours). A specialist cement and lime remover for marble, used with a floor brush and plenty of elbow grease, will eventually remove any excess cement.

Color Options

The two options shown here demonstrate perfectly the dramatic effects of contrast and atmosphere that can be achieved by changing the background colors from strong complementaries to a soothing pale tone.

- ☐ Cream
- ☐ Pumpkin
- ☐ Brown
- ☐ Light brown
- ☐ Mid gray
- ■ Charcoal

Autumnal colors against a pale background create a striking contrast which is stylish and tasteful, but would not overwhelm the other decor in your room.

- ☐ White
- ☐ Pumpkin
- ☐ Brown
- ☐ Mid gray
- ☐ Mid green
- ■ Charcoal

The complementary border and background colors used here give this classic design a more contemporary feel.

The jewel-like colors and patterns of this dazzling box were inspired by the great Byzantine mosaics, where artisans used simple shapes and bright colors to great effect. Traditional gold smalti is very expensive. In this project the box has been covered in gold paper, which shows through the clear glass, giving the effect of shimmery gold tesserae. Stained glass has been used as an alternative to the more traditional colored smalti. If you cannot get hold of real stained glass, paint the undersides of clear glass pieces with special glass paints.

Materials

tracing paper
marking pen
shiny gold paper
epoxy resin
clear glass
stained glass
wooden box
white or yellow craft glue
spray adhesive
grout

Equipment

mask and safety glasses
scissors or craft knife
mosaic nippers
glass or tile cutters
palette knife
squeegee
sponge
lint-free cloth
toothpicks

Byzantine Box

Prepare your box

Enlarge and modify the design to fit the shape and size of your box. Cover the outside of the box with gold paper, carefully sticking it down with craft glue or spray adhesive. Smooth out any creases and make sure the edges are stuck down well. Trace and transfer the design onto the outside of the box and clearly mark the outlines with a marking pen (see Tip on p.57).

Cut your glass tesserae

Break up the tesserae into approximate sizes and keep the colors in separate piles. Be very careful when cutting the tesserae as glass is extremely sharp and can be dangerous—wear a mask and safety glasses while cutting and work outside if possible (see Tip on p.119). Stained glass can be cut in the same way as mirror or ordinary glass, using a glass scorer and glass cutters.

Start laying the tesserae

Work in a well ventilated room and stick the tesserae to the box with a small amount of epoxy resin adhesive. Begin working on the top of the lid—start at the outside edge and work inward. Use small mirror pieces to outline the edges of the shapes. Fill the shapes with stained glass, which can be nibbled into exact shape using mosaic nippers. Stick clear glass tesserae onto the gold paper to fill in the background—this is quite painstaking work, so use a toothpick to help create even spaces between the glass pieces. When the top is complete, work around the edges of the lid and allow it to dry while you work on the bottom section of the box.

| TIP Cover the box with gold shiny paper before you begin the mosaic. Stick it down with craft glue and smooth out any creases as you go along. Do not fold the paper over into the inside of the box as this will stop the lid from fitting properly; instead trim the paper at the edge and stick it down securely. Any color of paper can be used, but shiny or metallic paper is the most effective as it helps the light reflect back through the glass. Aluminum foil can also be used to achieve glittering results.

Fran Soler

Template

Key

-  Emerald stained glass
- Mirror glass
- Clear glass
- Orange stained glass
- Turquoise stained glass
- Ruby stained glass
- Purple stained glass

LID

SIDES

Complete the sides

When working on the bottom section, check that the pattern lines up with the pattern on the sides of the lid. Make sure that the tesserae do not come too high up the sides of the box and obstruct the lid. When all the tesserae have been glued in place, let the box dry for a couple of days—until all the glue is completely clear and dry.

Grout the box

Grout the mosaic using a dark colored grout, which will help to bring out the bright jewel-like colors of the tesserae. Wipe away any excess grout with a rubber squeegee and a damp sponge. Do not disturb the box until it is dry to the touch, then give it a final polish with a dry lint-free cloth.

Color
Options

Use an eclectic mix of glittering tesserae, sparkling glass and twinkling tiles in rich jewel-like colors to create dazzling effects on different boxes.

Stained glass:

- ■ Turquoise
- ■ Navy
- ■ Ruby
- ■ Purple
- ■ Emerald
- □ Mirror glass

Try this eye-catching combination of shining mirror and brilliant stained glass, together with any little glittery bits and pieces you have, to produce an irresistibly kitsch result.

Stained glass:

- ■ Purple
- ■ Navy
- ■ Ruby
- ■ Gold smalti
- □ White ceramic tile
- □ Mirror glass

The end result here has a completely different effect. The gorgeous colors of the stained glass are enhanced by the simple white tesserae surround.

MEXICAN INSPIRATIONS

The complex history of Mexican civilization and culture can be traced back at least three thousand years. Many ancient artifacts still survive to this day, a testament to the highly skilled artisans and great craftsmanship of ancient Mexican civilization. These different cultures, emerging at separate times throughout early history, were linked not so much geographically, but by the shared beliefs in powerful gods and the striking similarities between art and rituals, as depicted in the many examples of carving and inscriptions.

Mosaics by Juan O'Gorman on the exterior of the University Library in Mexico City depict traditional Aztec and Mayan symbols.

Ancient Aztec ritual and ceremonial objects were often inlaid with turquoise, a highly valued stone, as seen on this mythological serpent.

Earliest examples of pottery date back to around 2000 B.C.—simple figurines and basic pots and cooking vessels from South Eastern Mesoamerica. Jade and stone carvings from the Olmec period (1200–400 B.C.) have also been discovered, as have many fine examples of pottery figurines from the Classic Veracruz period (A.D. 300-1200), Huaxtec stone sculptures (A.D. 900–1450), Mayan inscriptions and architecture (250 B.C.–A.D. 1000), Mixtec metalwork (A.D. 1200–1521) and Aztec mosaics (A.D. 1300–1521). Mayan and Aztec art have been very influential in the shaping of Mexican art as we know it today. Rediscovered in the nineteenth century, Mayan architecture and art have been much admired and are considered to be the most accomplished of ancient Mexican cultures. Detailed inscriptions and carvings inside tombs relate to major historical events and help to explain beliefs and time cycles of the Mayan period. Aztec art, although vibrant and full of life, appears obsessed with death—masks of human and animal skulls, sacrificial knives, and depictions of demons and warriors all show a preoccupation with horror and combat. But it was an era where the arts and crafts were greatly encouraged, and much of the work

This fragment of ancient Inca fabric shows how strong colors and bold motifs have always played a role in the decotrative arts of South America.

involved the use of gold and cut, polished jade, with turquoise and other precious stones used to create fabulous mosaics.

Before the Spanish conquest in 1520, gold- and silversmiths were held in very high regard, for their skill at inlaying and encrusting rings, necklaces and mosaics in exquisite detail. Much of the work was destroyed in the years following the conquest and many of the skills were replaced with new ideas imported by the Spanish. Tin glazed tiles were introduced to the Mexicans by the Spanish, who in turn had learned their skills from the Moors of Spain. Before the arrival of the Spanish, Mexican pottery had been limited to unglazed earthenware, fired only at a very low temperature, producing dull tiles by comparison. Not surprisingly, the Mexicans were dazzled by these incredible colors and their new found knowledge, and so took up the challenge of decorating the Spanish Catholic churches with enthusiasm. Two incredible churches from this era still survive today: Santa Maria Tonatzintla and San Francisco Atapec, both notable for their elaborate facades that are intricately decorated in joyful, uplifting colors using tiles made locally in Puebla—an important center for the manufacturing of tiles during colonial times. The Catholic church became a rich source of inspiration—imagery and devotion to the Virgin of Guadalupe (the patron saint of Mexico) was, and still is, used innumerable times by artists.

Mexico won independence from the Spanish in 1821, and the following years until the revolution of 1910 were a time of much political upheaval and social redress. A later period of renaissance, saw a resurgence of the fine arts, with artists such as Frida Kahlo, Diego Rivera, Jose Clemente Orozco and David Alfaro Siqueiros leading the way. Rivera, an influential muralist, received commissions for frescoes from the government and attempted to create a style reflecting both the history of Mexico and the socialist spirit of the revolution. Siqueiros, another muralist, made cartoons for the mosaics of the "rectorado" building at the University in Mexico City. Also at the university, covering the exterior of the library building, is a mosaic by Juan O'Gorman depicting Mayan hieroglyphics and Aztec motifs.

Today, art and color are an essential part of popular culture and life in Mexico, and modern day folk art and crafts are more likely to be found in markets and in people's homes, rather than in galleries.

Themes

religious icons, rituals, the day of the dead

Symbols

animals, birds, suns, snakes, skeletons, skulls

Materials

jade, turquoise, stone, ceramic, tin, bronze

Objects

textiles, masks, pottery, dolls, tiles

Places

churches, Palenque, Tulum, Monte Alban, Mexico City

The natural world can also provide you with inspiration—look at unusual plants and natural forms for interesting shapes, textures, colors and contrasts.

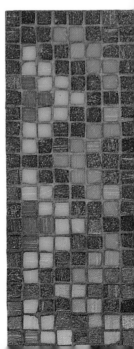

The combination of many different kinds of tesserae in this picture has created a wonderful effect. The use of fiery colors and the choice of stained glass for the sun against the vibrant blue of the sky combine to give off a feeling of shimmering light and heat rising from the arid landscape. There are endless possibilities for creating interesting combinations of tesserae in a project such as this. Use a mixture of terracottas, unglazed tiles, floor tiles, mirror pieces, ceramic, pebbles and bright shards of stained glass.

Cactus Wall Panel

Materials
tracing paper
marking pen
ceramic tiles
vitreous glass tesserae
stained glass
sturdy wooden board
white or yellow craft glue
tile adhesive
grout

Equipment
mask and safety glasses
glass or tile cutters
mosaic nippers
palette knife or small trowel
squeegee
rubber gloves
sponge and scourers
lint-free cloth

Prepare your design
Prepare the board by sanding away any sharp edges and applying a solution of craft glue and water (1 part glue: 4 parts water). Draw or trace the design onto the wood and clearly define the outline with a marking pen. Mark the basic colors in the appropriate sections.

TIP Place a sheet of tracing paper over the template. You can make the template any size so that the panel will fit comfortably in your wall space. Using a hard lead pencil, draw over the outline of the design. Turn the tracing paper over and rub over the outline with a soft lead pencil. Turn the paper over again and place it onto the wooden board, securing it with masking tape. Use the hard lead pencil to re-draw over the outline, pressing hard so that the pencil marks on the reverse side leave an outline on the board. Define the outline clearly with a marking pen.

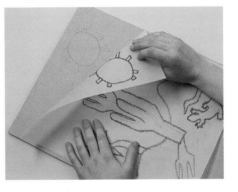

Mix your colors
Cut up the tesserae. Mix together tesserae of different materials, shapes and sizes, and of varying shades of the same color. Pile these together to be selected at random as you go along, but keep different colors separate. Trim the tesserae to the exact size required with the mosaic nippers.

Build up the picture
Working in the direct method, stick the tesserae onto the board with the tile adhesive—spread only a little at a time to avoid drying out before use. Work on one section of the image at a time, doing the details and foreground first, and the background later. Place tesserae of different materials next to each other: stained glass next to ceramic tile or next to vitreous glass, for example, to give texture and variety to the surface.

Katy Hall

Complete the background

When laying the background tesserae, graduate the tones of the tesserae as they become nearer to the sun, to give a sense of heat rising. Bring warm tones into the sand and outline the lizard with small dark tesserae to really make its shape stand out. When all the tesserae are in place, let the mosaic dry flat for a couple of days.

Apply the grout

Mix up a light brown grout in a bucket and spread over the mosaic using a small trowel or palette knife. Wipe off excess grout with a squeegee and smooth away any rough edges.

Clean up the panel

Clean off any remaining grout with a damp sponge—use a scourer for any stubborn spots—and polish with a dry lint-free cloth when the grout is dry to the touch.

Key

A mixture of pale and mid blue stained glass, with turquoise, navy blue, cobalt blue, pale blue, mid blue vitreous glass and ceramic

Brown and bronze ceramic and vitreous glass

A mixture of pale, bright and dark yellow, red, orange, ocher, sand-color, gold, and stone-color ceramic and vitreous glass

A mixture of dark green, mid green, and moss green vitreous glass and ceramic

Black ceramic

Template

Color Options

Experiment with combinations of different textured tesserae. Try rough, unglazed tiles for the sand against smooth shiny blues for the sky to add an extra dimension. You could also add a few multicolored pieces of crockery for extra interest within the details.

This assortment of hot colors and use of light-reflective tesserae help to create an atmosphere charged with intense heat.

Various shades of yellow and orange ceramic

Unglazed terracotta

Various shades of red, purple and violet ceramic

Black ceramic

Turquoise stained glass

Navy blue ceramic

Emerald ceramic

Grass green ceramic

White ceramic

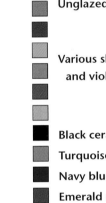

Various shades of yellow and orange and red ceramic

Black ceramic

Grass green ceramic

Emerald ceramic

Violet ceramic

Blue ceramic

Brown

White ceramic

Simply changing the colors around gives a completely different look while still retaining a sun-baked sensation.

This Mexican-inspired fireplace is made up of an amazing assortment of broken ceramic tiles, colored and patterned tiles and pieces of broken pottery. The foreground and background are clearly defined by the use of different color grouting and contrasting tesserae. The beauty of this project is that the colors and patterns of the tesserae bring the fireplace to life without the need for cutting them into precise shapes.

Mexican Fireplace

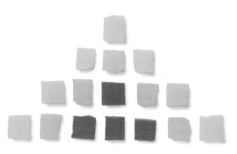

Materials
white ceramic tiles
black and white ceramic
multicolored and multi-patterned broken pottery
thin cardboard
double-sided or masking tape
white or yellow craft glue
cement
red cement dye

Equipment
mask and safety glasses
tile cutters
mosaic nippers
trowel
coarse sandpaper
scissors
craft knife
bucket
rubber gloves
sponge and scourers

Plan your design
Prepare the surface of the fireplace. If the surface is highly polished, rough it up by rubbing with coarse sandpaper, then brush away any loose dust before applying a solution of craft glue and water (1 part glue: 4 parts water). Draw the outline of the design with a strong black marking pen directly onto the surface.

Prepare your tesserae
Cut up tesserae into approximate shapes and sizes using the tile cutters and mosaic nippers. For the details you will need only white, and black and white ceramic pieces —this helps to make the distinction between the shapes and the background in the over-all effect. Place the tesserae in a container or on an old plate so that they are easily accessible when it comes to laying them into the cement.

Start on one section
Choose one shape to start with and sepa-rate it by building a cardboard wall (see Tip). Mix up a small amount of cement in a bucket, carefully following the manu-facturer's instructions and adding a little red cement dye to the mixture. Pour the cement into the walled-off section, and then place the tesserae into position. Select them at random and don't worry too much about getting the pieces to fit exactly—the cement plays a big part in the design, so uneven spaces are fine. You will need to work in short, fast bursts to stop the cement from setting before the tesserae are laid, so enlisting a helpful assistant here would be a great advantage. As you go along clean off any excess cement from the surface of the tiles with a damp sponge. Any stubborn lumps should be quickly rubbed off with a scouring pad.

Finish the other shapes
When all the tesserae are in place allow the piece to dry and move on to the next shape, where the process is repeated in the same way. Complete all the details and then allow them to dry for a couple of days to give the cement time to set thoroughly. When the cement is dry, carefully remove the card-board walls.

Steve Wright and Donald Jones

TIP In order to work on one section at a time, because the cement dries so quickly, build cardboard walls to make divisions. Use thin flexible cardboard and cut it into long strips. Using a craft knife, score along the length of the card, about 1½in (4cm) from one side and bend along this line. Stick the card around the area to be grouted with double-sided or masking tape. Press down securely to make sure the grout does not seep under the wall.

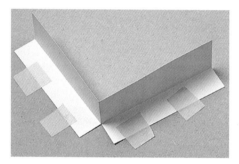

A cardboard wall

Fill in the background

Work on the background in small sections—separated by cardboard walls—in the same way. Apply the cement in small amounts using a trowel and then stick down pieces of multicolored broken pottery at random. Again, do not worry too much about making the pieces fit exactly—the broken ceramic and pottery pieces with all their varying colors and patterns do not need to have regular spacing between them to make them look amazing.

Template

Key

White patterned pottery

A mixture of bright multicolored pottery and patterned ceramic

Blue paint on wood surround

Red cement background

Color
Options

Don't be afraid of using unusual combinations of brightly colored broken pottery, multicolored and patterned tiles. Be daring—mix contrasting and complementary colours with bold background colors and bright grouting.

☐	White ceramic
▨	Blue and white willow pattern pottery
▨	Blue stained glass
▨	Ultramarine paint on wood surround
■	Black grout around details
▨	Cement grouted background

In this version the colors and materials have been limited to create a simpler and more toned-down result.

The addition of a few carefully placed pieces of mirror glass will reflect the flickering light from the fire and enliven the design.

☐	Yellow ceramic
☐	Mirror glass
▨	Red pottery
☐	Yellow paint on wood surround
☐	White grouted background
▨	Blue grout around details

The idea for this panel was inspired by an ancient Aztec turquoise serpent. The original serpent is believed to have been the decoration on a headdress. In this version, however, the serpent is nearly 10 feet long—a little too big to wear on a hat. While the original Aztec version of this snake is made up of turquoise stone, in this version ceramic tiles have been used. Various shades and thicknesses of the tiles give the serpent its texture and the triangular mirrored pieces create a snakeskin effect.

Aztec Serpent Wall Panel

Materials

tracing paper
wood
white or yellow craft glue
water
mirror
ceramic tiles
acrylic paint
grout (powdered)

Equipment

jigsaw
mask and safety glasses
tile or glass cutters
mosaic nippers
palette knife
rubber gloves
paintbrush
clean, dry cloth

Fran Soler

Prepare your base

Enlarge the design to the required size and trace it onto the wood. This design will work well in any size. The serpent pictured is nearly 10 feet (3m) long, however, which is not a practical size for most domestic environments. Unless the room is large enough to accommodate it, and there is sufficient distance from which to view the work, a smaller version would be much more suitable. Using a jigsaw, carefully cut the wood following the outline of the design. Prepare the surface of the wood by applying a craft glue and water solution (1 part glue: 4 parts water) with a large paintbrush.

Cut your tesserae

Cut the tiles into approximate sizes; these can be nibbled into shape later. To create the turquoise color use a mixture of blue and green tiles. To make sure of an even distribution of the various shades of tesserae, cut equal amounts of each of the different tiles and mix them together in a pile.

Lay the colored tesserae

Using the direct method, start from the outside edge and work inward, selecting tesserae at random from the pile. Stick them onto the wood using craft glue. If any of the tesserae need to be nibbled into more precise shapes, use the tile nippers. Carefully following the outline of the design, first apply all the blue and green tesserae, then the black for the eyes and white for the teeth. Let dry overnight—the outside edges need to be firmly set before you start working on the mirror sections so that the tesserae do not come off if the project is moved or leaned on.

Template

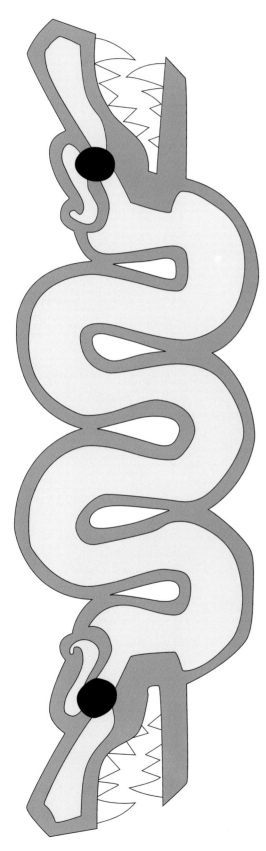

Add the mirror tesserae

Cut the mirror into small triangles. If you are working with a large sheet of mirror, first cut it down into manageable sized squares, approximately 6 x 6in (15 x 15cm) and then into triangles. Mirror can be cut in the same way as ceramic tiles; first score a line across the surface, and then break the mirror using the mouth of the cutters. At this stage it is essential to wear gloves as the edges of the mirror triangles are extremely sharp. Stick them to the wood using craft glue. Don't worry too much about leaving uneven spaces between pieces, as in this project the grout itself plays a large part in the overall effect. When all the tesserae are in place, allow the mirror to dry thoroughly for a couple of days before grouting.

Grout the mosaic

There are two different colored grouts used in this project; terracotta for the ceramic and turquoise for the mirror sections. To color grout, mix up a solution of water and acrylic paint. Add this solution to powdered grout and mix in the usual fashion. Bear in mind that the color will be lighter when the grout dries out and more paint may need to be added to make the color stronger. It is worth doing a few samples before grouting the real thing. First grout the ceramic sections using a dark terracotta grout. Work from the outside edge inward,

being careful to stop at the edge of the mirror section. Apply the grout with a palette knife, pushing the grout into the openings. Wipe off any excess grout using a clean damp sponge. Let dry before repeating the process for the mirrored sections, this time using turquoise grout.

Paint the base

When the grout is dry to the touch, polish off any remaining grout with a dry cloth. Finally, paint the edge of the wooden base with an acrylic paint, mixed to the same color and shade as the terracotta grout.

TIP Color grout by adding dyes, pigment, or in this case ordinary acrylic paint. Mix up the paint and water to a thick consistency like molasses and add it to the powdered grout. At first the paint mixture tends to make the grout streaky, so keep on mixing until the color is even throughout. Remember that the color will be lighter when it dries so it is worth making up a sample beforehand to check the color.

Key

Ceramic tiles:

- Black
- White
- Cobalt
- Navy
- Patterned blue
- Blue
- Turquoise
- Mirror glass

Color Options

The strong colors and simple shape allow you space to concentrate on creating interesting and unusual textures by using a mixture of different thicknesses, shades and tones of tesserae.

■ Unglazed terracotta
■ Turquoise ceramic
■ Black unglazed ceramic
□ White ceramic

Using different textures of tesserae combined with complementary colors creates even greater distinction between the outline and the body of the serpent.

This use of unusual combinations of vivid colors in glossy ceramic have transformed a simple design into a vibrant abstract composition.

■ Purple ceramic
■ Orange ceramic
■ Red ceramic
■ Lime green ceramic

A combination of brightly colored recycled ceramic tiles, bold designs and uneven surfaces reflect the light and bounce color off this mosaic window box, inspired by Mexican decorative arts and crafts. Any combination of bright colors would look great for this project, or any pieces of broken pottery, plates, teacups—anything bright and cheerful with bold patterns; here's a chance to recycle things that you may once have broken.

Mexican Window Box

Materials
spackling compound
sandpaper
tracing paper
pencil
marking pen
white or yellow craft glue
tile adhesive
ceramic tiles
grout
rectangular terracotta planter

Equipment
trowel
paintbrush
mask and safety glasses
tile cutters
mosaic nippers
palette knife
bucket
squeegee
sponge
cloth

Prepare the surface
Prepare the surface of the planter by applying a solution of craft glue and water (1 part glue: 4 parts water) with a paintbrush. Allow to dry thoroughly. Often, terracotta planters have a raised decoration or pattern on them. If this is the case, fill in the ridges with spackling compound applied with a trowel or palette knife (see Tip). When the compound has dried, smooth the surface by rubbing with sandpaper, then re-apply the glue and water solution to help the mosaic stick on top of the spackling compound patches and allow it to dry out thoroughly once again.

TIP Fill in unwanted ridges and inlaid patterns with spackling compound. Push firmly into the grooves with a palette knife or small trowel, smoothing it down with a squeegee. Spackling compound is a very useful material for smoothing out surfaces and filling in holes—always make sure the surface is dry and dust-free before applying. When the compound has dried, smooth the surface by rubbing it with sandpaper, then apply more craft glue and water solution and allow it to dry thoroughly before doing the mosaic.

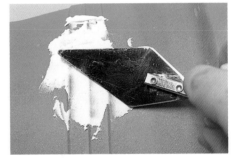

Break the tiles
Use the tile cutters to break the ceramic tiles into approximate sizes which can later be nibbled into exact shape when they are needed. Try to keep the colors in separate piles, particularly the greens and blues which are easily confused.

Apply the tiles
Stick the tiles to the sides of the planter with a small dab of tile adhesive. Some ceramic tile pieces have quite large bumps or grooves on the bottom, to help the grouting stick when they are being used as "whole" tiles, but when you are using them as mosaic material, these little bumps can make it hard to get the pieces to lie flat. In this project the tesserae don't need to be totally flat, but you can usually snip the bumps off using the mosaic nippers without causing too much damage.

Fran Soler

Complete the tiling

Work around the sides of the planter, one side at a time, leaving the ledge around the top until last so that you can pick up the pot easily to work on it. When all the tesserae are in place, allow it to dry for a couple of days before grouting.

Prepare the terracotta grout

Mix up a terracotta colored grout in a bucket. If you have plain white grout, add grout dye or pigment to the water before adding it to the powder. Dying grout to a convincing terracotta colour can be tricky— the grout has a tendency to dry pale pink if there is not enough dye in the mix. Make up a small test batch before starting on the real thing.

Grout the mosaic

Spread grout onto one side of the mosaic with a palette knife, pushing down firmly in between the spaces. Wipe off excess with a squeegee and move onto the next side. Continue all the way around until you are back at the beginning. Wipe a damp sponge all over the mosaic to take off any grout left on the surface. When the mosaic is dry to the touch, polish with a dry lint-free cloth. Allow to dry for a few days before planting.

Template

Key

Ceramic tiles:

Orange

Purple

Pale turquoise

Bright red

Turquoise

Bright yellow

Terracotta grout

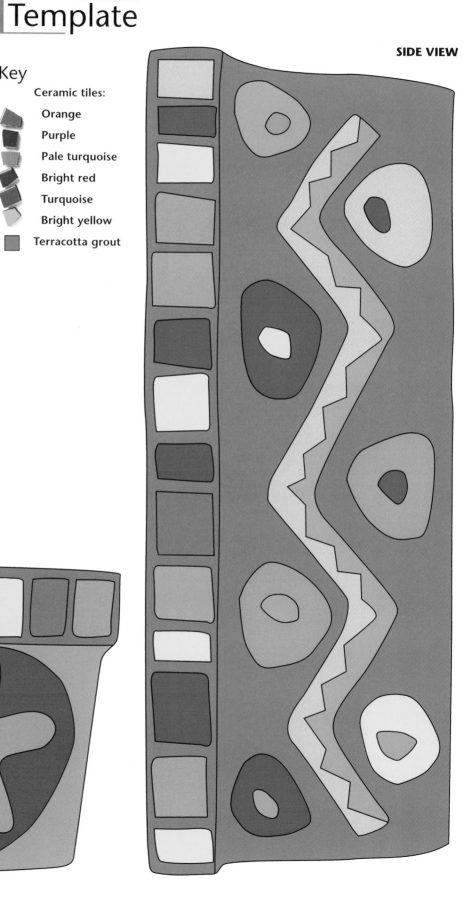

SIDE VIEW

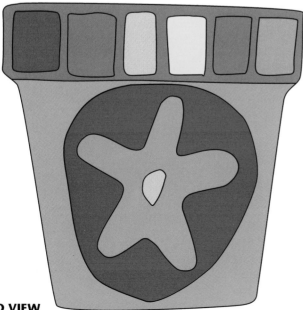

END VIEW

Color Options

Glazed ceramic tiles have been used to mosaic this lively window box, but you could add pieces of broken patterned china for detail, or unglazed ceramic for a more toned-down look.

- Bright green
- Bright pink
- Turquoise
- Lime green
- Bright red
- Cobalt blue
- Terracotta grout

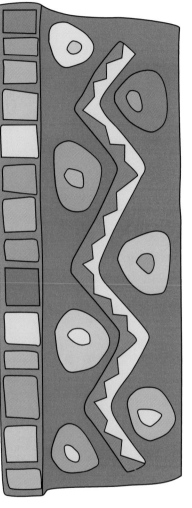

A mixture of shiny, bright tesserae in bold colors creates a warm, cheerful feeling that cannot fail to liven up your window ledge.

Go for pale colors for a cool look. Choose a combination of muted colors of similar intensities for this more sophisticated effect.

- Violet
- Turquoise
- Pale blue
- Sand color
- Sea green
- Cobalt blue
- Terracotta grout

ISLAMIC INSPIRATIONS

Islamic mosaics recall the work of the Byzantine era, in their use of lavish materials and intricate designs. Islamic mosaic makers used the medium to spectacular effect—usually as an architecturally related art form and often using pre-shaped colored tiles to create some of the most incredible mosaics ever seen. The main difference between styles is that in Byzantine art depictions of Christ and saints are an essential subject, while in Islamic art there is no place for the depiction of God, and abstract representations of natural forms, geometric patterns and inscriptions are applied instead.

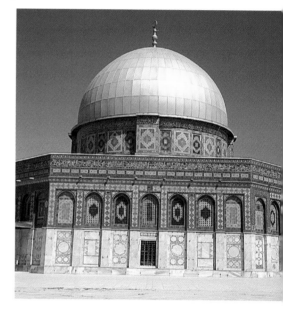

Intricate mosaics on a grand scale decorate the Haroun Mausoleum in Isfahan.

The foliage patterns and coloring of this Romanian kilim (below) show how the influence of Islamic textiles spread northwards through Eastern Europe.

The term "Islamic art" is a very loose one and covers a wide variety of styles, ages and applications—not only art related to the religion of Islam, but more the arts of all Islamic cultures. The height of Islamic civilization ran through the millennium from the seventh to the seventeenth century, fitting into the period between the collapse of the Roman and Byzantine empires and the rise of the Western European nations. During this time, the Islamic nations of Syria, Egypt, Iraq and Iran prospered as the central players in intercontinental trade between the East and West. At first, textiles were the most significant of the arts, not only because the trade in textiles was very important economically, but also because before the wide-

This mosaic detail from the tenth-century Great Mosque at Cordoba shows both Arabic lettering and semi-abstract floral patterns.

With a dazzling gold roof and stunning mosaics, both inside and out, Jerusalem's Dome of the Rock (left) dates from 692.

Themes

religion, geometry, repeat patterns

Symbols

inscriptions, trees, plants

Materials

marble, ceramic, smalti, enamel, stone, gold

Objects

books, rugs, textiles, tiles

Places

JERUSALEM
The Dome of the Rock

SPAIN
The Great Mosque of Cordoba

IRAN
Shah Mosque, Isfahan

spread use of paper, textiles provided a way of transferring and spreading ideas between regions. Islamic textiles provide a rich source of inspiration for mosaicists, with the patterns of handwoven rugs made up of small blocks of color, that are in many ways comparable to mosaics. The book also played a central role in Islamic arts, being the most culturally important because of the writing of God's words, and books were beautifully illustrated with fantastic paintings. The significance of writing overflowed into other arts, inscriptions decorated everything from carvings to buildings. Other important arts such as ceramics, glass, metalwork, carved rock crystal and ivory all show the same symbols.

The Dome of the Rock, set on the site of Jerusalem's Temple Mount where Solomon's temple had once stood, was built in the late seventh century. Often considered the first work of Islamic architecture, this incredible eight-sided building was once entirely covered with mosaics. The exterior mosaics were replaced with tiles in the sixteenth century, but the interior remains almost intact. The lower walls are covered in luxurious marble, cut and fitted into intricate patterns. Around the top of the arcade of the inner facade are beautifully inscripted words, the earliest known evidence for the written text of the Koran. The upper walls of the octagon and the drum are covered in a mosaic of dazzling colors and gilded glass tesserae. Most of the decorations represent flowers, plants, trees, jewels and chalices; what would once have been used as border or background elements in Byzantine mosaics now became the central subject of the decorations. Another important Islamic building is the Great Mosque of Cordoba, once the capital of Muslim Spain, which was built with workmen and materials from Constantinople and elaborately decorated with gold glass mosaic and carved marble. The Shah Mosque in Isfahan is also notable for its incredible decoration. The walls are covered with multicolored glazed tiles, and the entrance portal is decorated with a fantastic mosaic made up of seven colors of ceramic tiles which have been cut into size from larger tiles— a fairly common technique for architectural mosaics but none-the-less one of the most stunning examples in existence.

Cool colors, smooth textures and intricate patterns swirl around this table top, inspired by wonderful Islamic geometric patterns and early ceramics, which were often painted cobalt or turquoise blue.

Geometric Table Top

Materials

tracing paper
pencil and marking pen
plywood (5 ply)
white or yellow craft glue
ceramic plates with blue willow pattern
vitreous glass tesserae
matt ceramic tesserae
sand
cement
table base

Equipment

mask and safety glasses
tile cutters
mosaic nippers
craft knife
squeegee
rubber gloves
bucket
cloths
screwdriver

Prepare the base

Enlarge the design to fit the size of your table top with the help of a photocopier. Draw or trace the design onto the wooden board and define the outline clearly with a marking pen. Prepare the surface of the wood (see Tip).

Begin the central swirls

Use mosaic nippers to cut the tesserae to size. When working on curves, nip the edges off the two bottom corners to taper the

TIP Another way of preparing a wooden surface before doing a mosaic is to score lines with a sharp craft knife, making deep scratches in a crisscross pattern. Particleboard will need to be sealed with a craft glue and water solution (1 part glue: 4 parts water) after scoring. The deep scored lines give the grout or cement fixative something extra to grip on to.

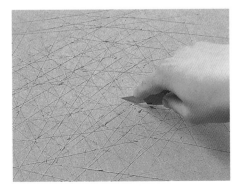

shape—this helps to make the tesserae flow along the curve. Begin with the central swirls in a strong dark color first, sticking the tesserae firmly into place with a small dab of craft glue applied to the back of the tile. Outline the swirls with a row of randomly selected pale blues and willow pattern background tesserae.

Continue the mosaic around the outside edge, using bolder, darker blue tesserae and some willow pattern tesserae. On the inside edge of this border, follow the curve with a mixture of paler blues and willow pattern in a continuous line—the same colors that are to be used for the background.

Complete the background

Following the direction of the pattern shown on the template, build up the background so the tesserae flow in curved lines. The tesserae can be chosen at random, but try to achieve a certain amount of balance between the various blue shades and the willow pattern. Finish the edge of the table top by firmly sticking tesserae all the way around the side of the board. When all the tesserae are affixed, allow the table top to dry for a couple of days before grouting.

Norma Vondee

Make the sand and cement mixture

Wearing heavy-duty rubber gloves, slowly add water to a mixture of sand and cement (3 parts sand: 1 part cement) in a bucket until the mixture has a crumbly, moist consistency. Add a little cement dye at this stage if you need to. Spread the sand and cement mixture over the surface of the mosaic with a squeegee, firmly pressing down so that the mixture fills all the spaces, and smooth around the rim of the table top so there are no sharp edges. Wipe the mosaic with a wet cloth to remove any excess sand and cement mixture. Repeat with a damp cloth to make sure all the excess has been smoothed away and finally polish with a dry cloth.

Allow the cement mix to set

The sand and cement mixture will take a couple of days to cure. Allow the table top to dry in a cool room with a slightly damp cloth over the mosaic surface. Do not let the cloth dry out—place a plastic sheet loosely over the top and check every now and then that the cloth is still damp.

Join the top to the base

After a couple of days the table top will be ready. Join the table base securely to the bottom and you are ready to go.

Template

Key

- Willow pattern pottery
- Cobalt unglazed ceramic
- Dark blue vitreous glass
- Speckled blue unglazed ceramic
- Pale blue unglazed ceramic
- White unglazed ceramic

Color Options

Create a strong contrast between foreground and background with the use of bold colors for the swirls against pale colors and subtle patterned tesserae.

☐ A mixture of black and pale
☐ gray vitreous glass, white
☐ and gray patterned pottery,
☐ and off-white unglazed
☐ ceramic
■ Black unglazed ceramic

Here the strong contrasts between black, white and gray produce a dramatic and eye-catching design. You could also paint the base to complement the table top.

☐ A mixture of flowery
☐ patterned pottery, white
☐ and pale ocher unglazed
☐ ceramic, and yellow and
☐ orange vitreous glass
☐
■ Terracotta unglazed ceramic

Minute, flower-patterned tesserae for the swirl shape, with a mixture of yellow, ocher and terracotta for the background, create a warm earthy feel. Use a combination of shiny and matte tesserae to create a textured finish.

Islamic Pattern Wall Panel

Materials
graph paper
lead pencils
colored pencils
marking pen
tracing paper
vitreous glass tesserae
white or yellow craft glue
particleboard squares
grout

Equipment
mask and safety glasses
mosaic nippers
paintbrush
scourer
trowel
sponge
bucket
cloths
squeegee

This intricately patterned panel was designed and made by the students of Stoke Newington Secondary School, in London, where Susan Goldblatt taught as Artist-in-Residence. Working in small groups, the students studied Islamic rugs, tiles and textiles for inspiration and ideas before working together in their designs. Each member of each group participated in designing and making the mosaic sections, creating a stunning wall panel for the whole school to enjoy.

TIP It is always easier to work out geometric patterns on graph paper. Mark out the outline of the outer edge with a bold marking pen, and draw out the design in pencil first until satisfied with it, then define the pattern with the marking pen. The grid of the graph paper will help to guide the drawing and make it easier to create a symmetrical design.

Design the sections
Design each of the sections on graph paper, keeping in mind that they will be joined together to make a whole image later on, so consider the balance of geometry and symmetry throughout. Enlarge each section separately using a photocopier and color in the designs with colored pencils. Limit the amount of colors in the design to about five or six and use the same ones for each section—this will create a sense of continuity throughout the panel.

Apply glue to particleboard
Prepare the surface of the particleboard by applying a solution of white or yellow craft glue and water (1 part glue: 4 parts water) with a paintbrush. Make sure that all of the particleboard sections are of equal size so that the panel fits together when assembled.

Transfer design onto wood
Trace the designs onto the wood. Mark the outlines clearly with a marking pen and write the colors in the appropriate places.

Susan Goldblatt

Template

Key

Vitreous glass:

White

Pale Green

Dark red

Charcoal

Black

Blue

Stick down tesserae

Cut the tesserae to the exact sizes required using the mosaic nippers. Be wary of flying shards of glass as you cut and be sure to wear protective glasses and a mask. Stick the tesserae into position by applying a small dab of craft glue to the ridged bottom of the tesserae—the smooth flat side of the tesserae being the top surface. When all the tesserae are in place, allow them to dry overnight before grouting.

Grout the mosaic

In a bucket, mix up a dark grout according to the manufacturer's instructions. Spread the grout over the surface of the mosaic with a trowel, pushing the grout well down into the spaces. Smooth the surface with a squeegee to remove any lumps. Wipe the mosaic with a damp sponge to take off any remaining grout and polish with a dry cloth when the grout is dry to the touch. Scrub off any stubborn traces of grout with a scouring pad.

Assemble and attach mosaic to wall

When all the sections are completed and the grout has dried thoroughly, assemble the sections together and affix to a large backing board with strong adhesive. Make sure the adhesive has dried thoroughly before attaching it securely to the wall.

Color
Options

These templates show just one of the sections which make up the whole panel. The colors shown for each option can be used in any combination for the other panels— let your imagination take over!

Ceramic tiles:

- Ocher
- Turquoise
- Sky blue
- Dark green
- White

Use simple colors as found in nature to create a rich composition with forest greens and oceanic blues.

Ceramic tiles:

- Red
- Mid green
- Ocher
- Purple
- Orange

For a modern, jazzy look, go for complementary colors in bright tones which will enliven the complex patterns to truly dazzling effect!

The inspiration for this box came from looking at kilims and carpets, with their beautiful colors and intricate patterns. Interlocking geometric shapes flow around the sides of the box and, as this is a repeating pattern, the design can be made longer or shorter, expanded or compressed to fit any shape.

Kilim Pencil Box

Materials
wooden box
graph paper
tracing paper
pencils
marking pen
white or yellow craft glue
tile adhesive
grout
vitreous glass tesserae

Equipment
mosaic nippers
paintbrush
sandpaper
palette knife
mask and safety glasses
bucket
squeegee
sponge and dry cloth
scouring pad

Plan your design
Measure your box and draw the outline onto graph paper. Draw out a grid of ½in (1cm) squares within the shape. Using four different colored pencils, work out the design so it fits exactly into the outline. Give each of the colors a number and mark the squares accordingly. Take a sheet of tracing paper and carefully trace over the lines.

Prepare the box
Clean the surface of the box by sanding away any old paint or varnish with sandpaper. You can now transfer the drawing to the box. You might find it easier to do this by drawing directly onto the box using your drawing as a guide, as it can be very difficult trying to trace such small squares (see Tip on p.57). Carefully mark out the numbers of the colors in the squares with a marking pen. Apply a solution of craft glue and water (1 part glue: 4 parts water). Allow the box to dry thoroughly.

Start to apply the tesserae
While the box is drying, cut the tesserae into quarters using the mosaic nippers. Try to cut as squarely as possible, so that the edges can all line up. Take the lid of the box and begin working on the sides first. Spread a little tile adhesive onto the wood and firmly press the tesserae into

place with the flat surface facing upward. The tesserae also have beveled edges and these should line up along the top edge of the sides to guarantee an even edge between the top of the lid and the sides.

TIP When sticking tesserae to a lidded box it is essential to align the tesserae in such a way that the lid can be opened and closed easily, without creating an unnatural space between the tesserae of the lid and the base. You will need to cut your tesserae to a size that fits neatly into the box size. Vitreous glass tesserae have a beveled edge around the underside, which will ensure a clean join at the corners of the box. If you are cutting your tesserae to a small size, make sure you place them the right way round so that the beveled edges meet at the corners.

Richard Hanson

Template

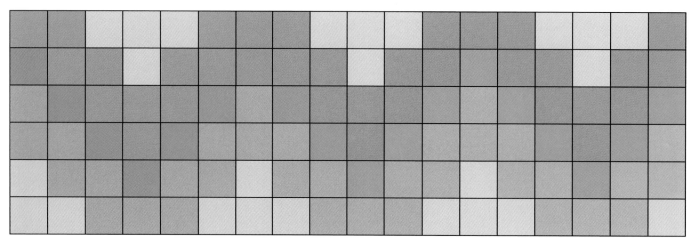

TOP VIEW

SIDE VIEW

Work slowly and methodically around the sides of the lid, placing the tesserae very closely together. Allow to dry thoroughly before beginning to work on the top of the lid—put the tesserae on the bottom section of the box while it is drying. Once all sections of the box are covered in mosaic, let the project dry thoroughly overnight.

Grout the box
Mix up a fine dark grout and apply with a palette knife, pushing down well into the spaces. Wipe off any excess grout with a squeegee and a wet sponge. If any stubborn grout remains on the surface, scrub with a scouring pad and water. When the grout is dry to the touch, polish with a dry lint-free cloth.

Key

Vitreous glass:

Purple-gray

Sea green

Cobalt blue

Fawn

END VIEW

Color
Options

All you need for this design is four different colors of tesserae. You could combine different types of tesserae, for example, a mixture of glazed and unglazed ceramic, but do try to use the same thickness to ensure an even surface.

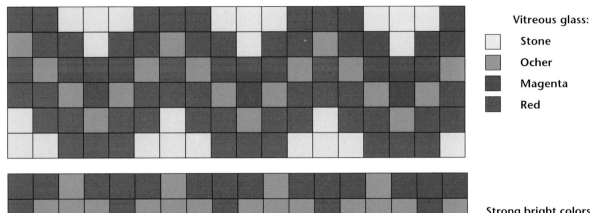

Vitreous glass:

Stone

Ocher

Magenta

Red

Strong bright colors set against pale, neutral colors produce striking results, as shown here. Choose a dark-colored grout to enhance the tesserae.

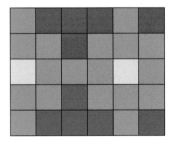

Vitreous glass:

Blue-gray

Rose pink

Mid gray

Moss green

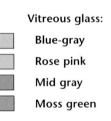

Harmonious colors in pastel tones produce a mellow effect, with a pale grout between to further define the tones.

With a civilization and culture stretching back for thousands of years, the Eastern world offers vast scope for inspiration and ideas. Many objects were made for religious and practical reasons rather than purely esthetic, with artists and craftsmen following strict guidelines and using traditional skills to create outstanding artwork of symbolic and spiritual significance.

EASTERN
INSPIRATIONS

Traditional Eastern motifs of dragonflies, flowers and reeds have been used to decorate this nineteenth-century porcelain vase from Saigon.

Religion, and in particular Buddhism, plays a major role in the history of Eastern art. Originally founded in India, Buddhism was introduced to China and Japan by Indian merchants, followers of the teachings of Siddharta (later known as Buddha), who was born in Nepal around 560 B.C. Buddha appears time and time again as a central feature in Indian art, with paintings and other objects of artwork being used as icons of worship. Artists and craftsmen combined intricate detailing, intense color and the use of religious and spiritual symbolism to create the essential elements of Indian art. This was expressed in many forms—cave-shrines, paintings, ornamental carvings, bronze figures of Buddha, sculptures of Hindu gods and lavishly decorated temples and palaces. Colored glazed tiles used were developed in Lahore, around the beginning of the seventeenth century, and used to adorn buildings with bright, abstract flower and figure designs.

Religion, superstition, astrology and mythology play a very large part in the history of Chinese civilization. Ancient China had three main religions: Confucianism, Taoism and Buddhism, each of the three having different values, while at the same time complementing each other. Confucianism gives the individual a commitment to social order, Taoism gives him a place on earth and Buddhism gives him a hope in a future life. Although the

These Japanese origami papers use traditional designs, such as the over-lapping wave pattern, but with bright, modern colors.

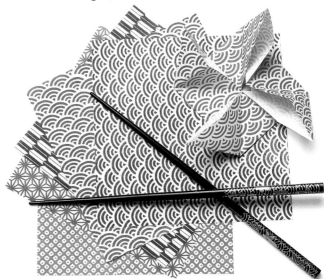

Natural materials such as feathers and insects' wings have been used to decorate this eighteenth-century fan.

ancient Chinese did not have much use for myths, later on mythological creatures such as the dragon, the phoenix and the unicorn became popular in the retelling of stories and appear over and over again in paintings, textiles and other art forms. The Chinese excelled in all disciplines of craftsmanship, creating magnificent bronze cast vessels, lacquerwork and textiles, becoming famous for outstanding porcelain around the middle of the sixteenth century.

The first major religion of ancient Japan was Shinto. Based on nature, sacred beings known as "kami" were worshipped, as well as mountains, streams, rocks and trees. Shinto shrines and temples were very simple, often single empty rooms raised off the ground on wooden stilts, with no elaborate decoration, as this was frowned upon. Buddhism reached Japan via China in the sixth century A.D., along with elaborate rituals and temples, which were highly decorated and richly ornamental—in contrast to the simple Shinto temples. Under the influence of Zen Buddhists, gardening evolved into an art form. These beautifully designed gardens contained bonsai trees, volcanic rocks, mosses, ponds, streams and pathways, set out to symbolize aspects of nature and evoke an atmosphere of peace and meditation. Japanese artists and craftsmen were highly skilled in metal casting, sword making, lacquerwork and miniaturization as well as creating outstanding paintings on silk and paper. Color and form were the essential elements and much of the painting represented different forms of nature and spirituality.

Although there is no tradition of mosaic making in the East, there is a vast wealth of ideas and subjects, art forms, textile designs and patterns from which to draw inspiration.

"Krishna tells his friend of his amorousness" in this richly colored eighteenth-century Indian book illustration.

Themes

Buddhism, Taoism, Confucianism, Shinto

nature, astrology, myths and legends, temples, palaces, thrones

Symbols

elephant, warrior, butterfly, dragon, unicorn, phoenix, dragonfly

Patterns

mountains, streams, waves, clouds, rocks, trees, flowers

Materials

wood, paper, silk, bronze, jade

Objects

lacquerwork, porcelain, textiles, kimonos, paintings, sculpture

Places

landscape gardens, palaces, shrines, temples

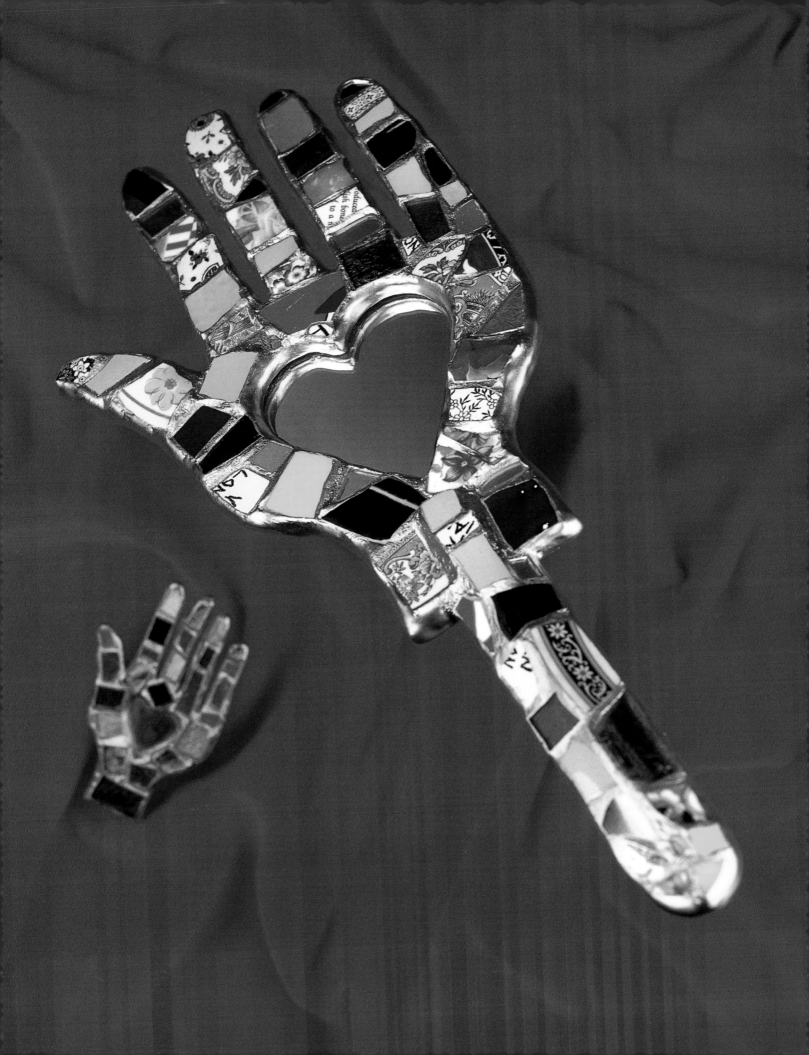

By combining simple techniques with complex shapes and fantastic colors, you can turn the ordinary into the extraordinary. Take this dazzling hand-held mirror by Steve Wright, which turns a simple idea for an everyday object into a work of art.

Hand-shaped Mirror

Materials
stained glass
mirror glass
wood
white or yellow craft glue
epoxy resin adhesive
white powdered grout
gold paint

Equipment
jigsaw
mask and safety glasses
glass scorer and cutter
mosaic nippers
palette knife
bucket
sponge
lint-free cloth
paintbrush
sandpaper

Prepare your base
Draw or trace the design onto the wood, clearly marking the outlines with a marking pen. Cut the shape out using a jigsaw (see Tip) and sand down any rough edges. Prepare the surface of the wood by applying a solution of white or yellow craft glue and water (1 part glue: 4 parts water). Allow to dry thoroughly.

TIP Clamp the wood securely to a workbench and use a saw to cut out the shape, following the design closely. It is much quicker and easier to use an electric jigsaw if you have one, but the same result can be achieved with a hand saw. Use sandpaper to smooth away any rough edges.

Cut and glue the tesserae
Break the tesserae using glass scorers and cutters. Nibble into the exact shape using the mosaic nippers. Wear a safety mask and glasses while doing this to avoid flying glass shards and work outside if possible. (See also Tip on p.119.)

Stick the tesserae into position with a small amount of epoxy resin. This stage needs to be completed outside or in a very well ventilated room as the adhesive gives off dangerous fumes. Let dry thoroughly before grouting (a few days should be enough).

Steve Wright

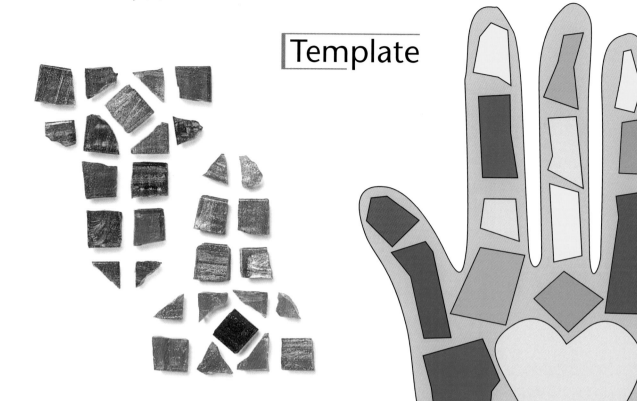

Template

Apply the grout

Grout the mosaic using a white or light colored grout; it doesn't really matter too much since the grout will later be painted, but light is better than dark. Push the mosaic down into the spaces with a palette knife and smooth away any sharp edges around the sides. Wipe away the excess with a damp sponge and polish when dry to the touch using a dry lint-free cloth.

Paint over the grout

When the mosaic is completely dry and the grout has thoroughly set—after about two or three days—paint over the grout with shiny gold acrylic paint. Let the mirror dry thoroughly for a couple of days before admiring your reflection.

Key

☐ Mirror glass

A mixture of patterned, yellow, orange, red, sky blue, dark blue, emerald, and turquoise ceramic and stained glass

☐ Bright gold grout

Color Options

Choose vibrant gem-like colors and sparkling tesserae to create a brilliant impression, or opt for a cool color scheme of subtle ceramic with pale grouting.

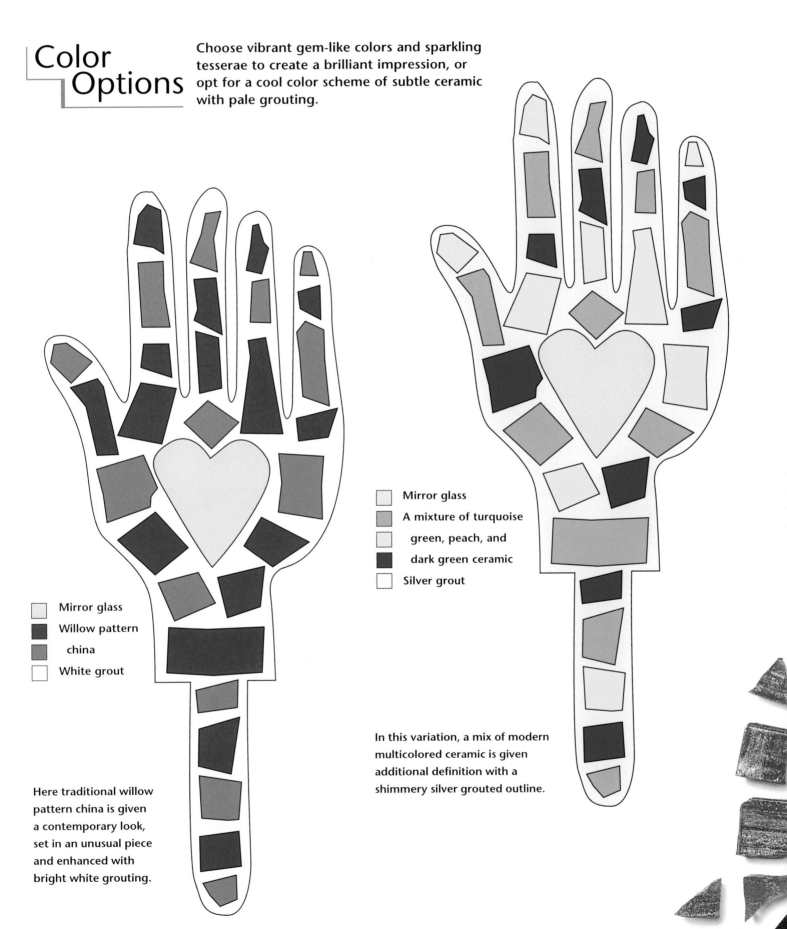

Mirror glass

A mixture of turquoise
green, peach, and
dark green ceramic

Silver grout

Mirror glass

Willow pattern
china

White grout

Here traditional willow pattern china is given a contemporary look, set in an unusual piece and enhanced with bright white grouting.

In this variation, a mix of modern multicolored ceramic is given additional definition with a shimmery silver grouted outline.

The unusual combination of materials in this mosaic creates a striking contrast between the bold spots and outlines of the body and the delicate wispy lines and iridescent colors of the stained glass wing segments.

Butterfly
Pot Stand

Materials
construction paper
pencil
plywood (5 ply)
white or yellow craft glue
stained glass
ceramic tesserae
vitreous glass tesserae
sand
cement

Equipment
mask and safety glasses
scissors
tile cutters
mosaic nippers
craft knife
squeegee
rubber gloves
bucket
cloths

Before you start
When preparing the plywood for this project there is no need to seal the surface with a craft glue solution—the scoring lines help the cement and sand grouting really stick fast to the wood. But, if you do choose to work onto particleboard, the surface will need to be sealed.

Prepare the design and tesserae
Draw or trace the design onto the wooden board and define the outlines clearly with a marking pen. Score the surface of the wood with a sharp craft knife, making deep scratches all over in a crisscross pattern. Break up the tiles and stained glass using the mosaic nippers, being extra careful when cutting the stained glass, as the shards can be extremely sharp.

Make the butterfly
Work on the butterfly detail first, sticking the pieces to the board with a small dot of craft glue. Nibble away at the corners of the square tesserae to make the round dots on the wings. The mosaic will flow better if you use the grain of the stained glass lengthwise through the segments.

TIP
Any shape or species of butterfly can be used for this design. Take a sheet of construction paper and fold it in half. Draw the outline of one half of a butterfly, the folded line being the point where the outline is divided in half. Cut out the shape with a sharp pair of scissors—the result is a perfectly symmetrical butterfly template to draw around.

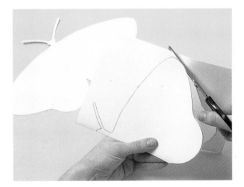

Norma Vondee

Template

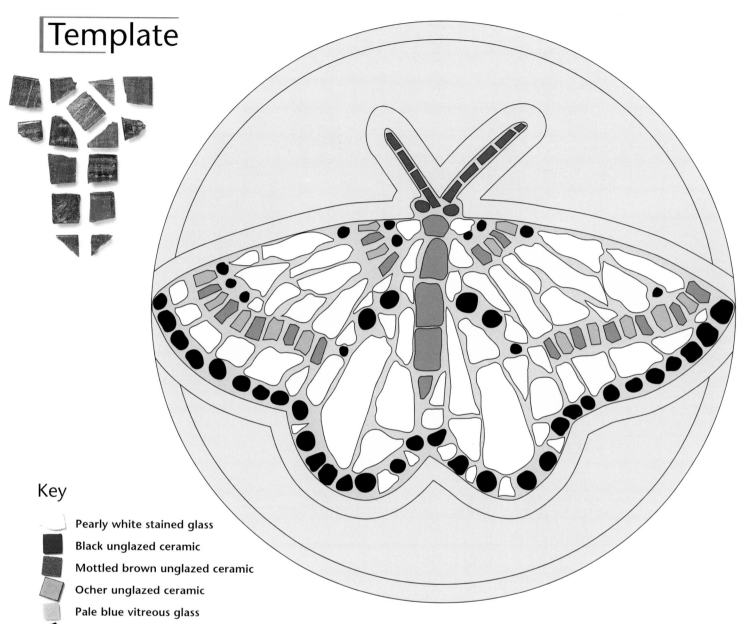

Key

Pearly white stained glass

Black unglazed ceramic

Mottled brown unglazed ceramic

Ocher unglazed ceramic

Pale blue vitreous glass

Black vitreous glass

Fill in the background

First, make an outline of the butterfly with the background color, then follow the curve of the outside edge, so the tesserae flow around the butterfly shape. When the background is complete, apply tesserae to the rim of the board and allow them to dry for a couple of days before grouting.

Make sand and cement mixture

In a bucket, slowly add a little water to a mixture of sand and cement (3 parts sand: 1 part cement), until the mixture is moist

and crumbly—not wet. At this stage you can add a little cement dye to get the color you require. Apply the sand and cement mixture with a squeegee, pressing down hard so the mixture fills in all the openings, and smooth around the edge of the rim so there are no sharp edges. Wipe the surface with a wet cloth, taking away all the excess sand and cement. Repeat the process with a moist cloth until all the excess has been smoothed away and then polish with a dry cloth.

Allow to dry

Let the project dry in a cool room. Place a slightly damp cloth over the mosaic and leave it alone for a couple of days to allow the cement to cure. Do not allow the cloth to dry out—make sure it stays moist by loosely covering with a plastic sheet.

Color Options

For maximum effect use the delicate strands of color within the stained glass to create veins running through the wings of the butterfly, and choose contrasting colors for the spots and patterns.

A mixture of pale ocher,

mottled stone and

white unglazed ceramic

A mixture of cobalt and

sky blue stained glass

Red vitreous glass

Black unglazed ceramic

This combination of natural shades of ocher, brown, and red, with the addition of a little shimmery stained glass, and highlights in red vitreous glass, give this piece a warm, earthy look.

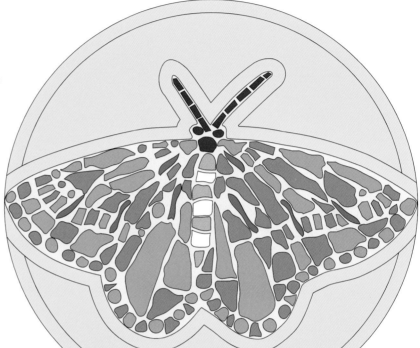

Pea green vitreous glass

A mixture of mottled brown

and black unglazed ceramic

A mixture of red and white

vitreous glass

Black stained glass

The use of a bright background color, bold butterfly details and an assortment of different textured tesserae combine to create a very striking impression.

Bright, sparkling stained glass tesserae are used to create the dragonfly, which stands out against the pale background, giving a sense of depth to this simply shaped vase. Any vase or pot can be transformed with mosaic, but the simple shapes always seem to work best.

Dragonfly Vase

Materials
ceramic vase
sandpaper
white or yellow craft glue
stained glass
ceramic tiles
grout
marking pen
emulsion paint

Equipment
tile cutters
glass scorer
mosaic nippers
paintbrush
mask and safety glasses
palette knife
squeegee
sponge
dry cloth

Remove glaze with sandpaper

Prepare the surface of the vase. In order for the tesserae to stick to the surface of the vase you will first need to rub off some of the glaze with sandpaper. It is not necessary to rub all the glaze off, just enough to make the surface slightly rough. Do not take off any of the glaze from the inside of the vase as this may make it leak. Sanding the glaze will give off quite a lot of very fine dust—work outside if possible and always wear a dust mask and safety glasses. Cover the surface with craft glue. If you are working on a vase that has a distinctive pattern, paint over this with white emulsion paint after the craft glue has dried. This will give you a blank canvas to work on and make marking the dragonfly design onto it easier. When the paint has dried, apply another layer of craft glue.

Transfer design onto vase

Draw or trace the dragonfly design onto the vase. Space the dragonflies evenly around the vase and mark the outlines clearly with a marking pen.

Begin with dragonfly details

Break up stained glass tesserae into approximate sizes. Begin with the dragonfly details. Use a round piece of stained glass for the head of a dragonfly and trim it into shape with the mosaic nippers. Stick the tesserae into place with a small amount of craft glue. The bodies and wings of the dragonflies should be built up with small tesserae to give a smooth flow around the curve of the vase. Add the grass rushes in the same way.

TIP Take a piece of square stained glass and use the mosaic nippers to nibble away at the corners. Keep on turning the piece around with one hand while nibbling at the edges with the other. Work all the way around until there are no corners left and the square becomes a round dot.

Claire Foss and Tipper Lewis

Fill in background

Use plain ceramic tiles to fill the background. Break tesserae into approximate sizes and nibble into exact shape using mosaic nippers. Again, the tesserae need to be fairly small so there are no bumps sticking out around the curve. When all the tesserae have been stuck into position, let the vase dry overnight before grouting.

Grout and smooth the mosaic

In a bucket, mix up a fine pale gray or silvery grout by adding a little dye to the water or using a pre-colored grout. Spread grout over the mosaic with a palette knife, pushing the grout well into the spaces between the tesserae. Remove any excess lumps with a rubber squeegee, and smooth around the curve of the vase making sure there are no sharp edges sticking out. Wipe the surface of the vase with a damp sponge to remove any remaining grout and polish with a dry cloth when the surface is dry to the touch.

Template

Key

	White ceramic
	Dark green stained glass
	Turquoise stained glass
	Red stained glass
	Orange stained glass
	Silver-gray grout

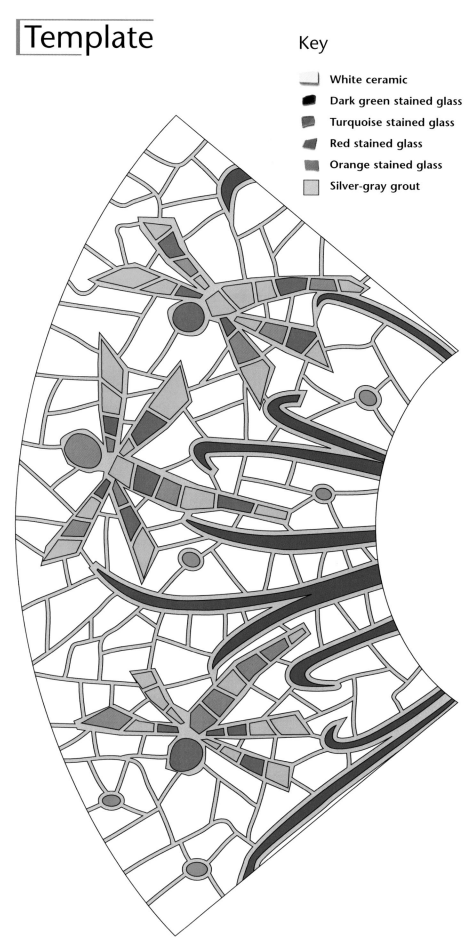

Color Options

Play around with different textures of tesserae—try using shiny or patterned pieces for the details against a background of matte muted tones to add definition and depth to the design.

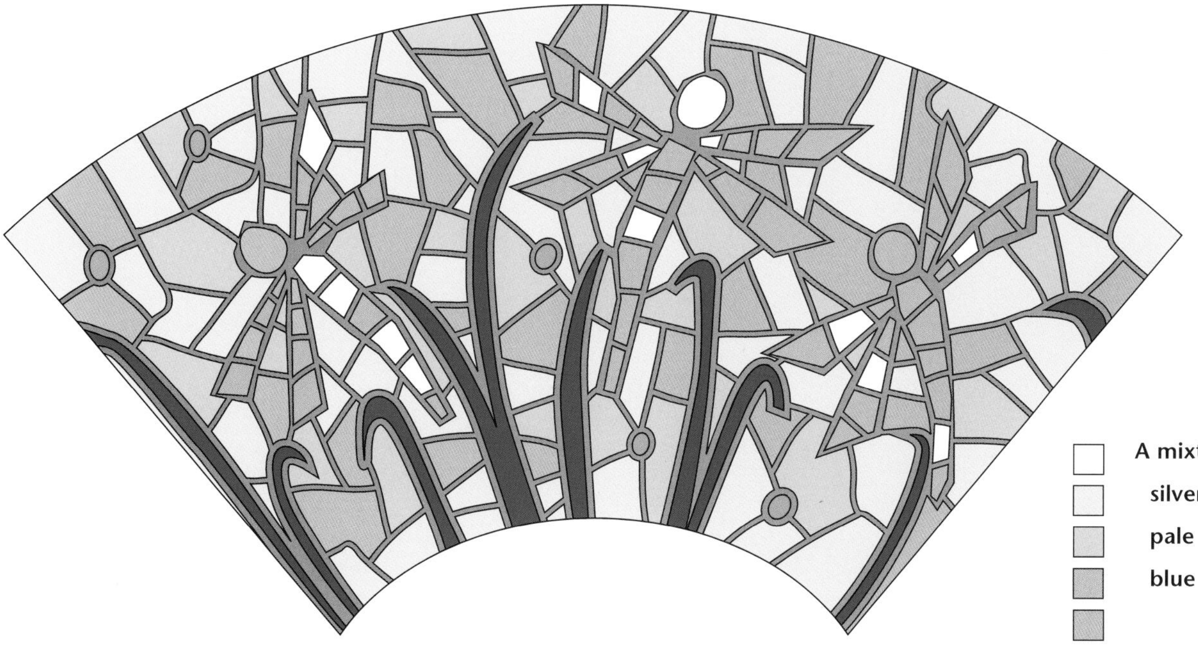

Create an elegant look using wispy stained glass for the dragonflies against a pale background of watery colors.

A mixture of white and
silver stained glass, with
pale blue, gray-blue, sky
blue vitreous glass

Pale pink stained glass
Orange stained glass
Dark green vitreous glass
Dark gray grout

A mixture of cream, off-white,
and pale gray ceramic

A mixture of bright red, yellow,
and turquoise broken crockery

Orange brocken crockery
Bright green ceramic
Charcoal grout

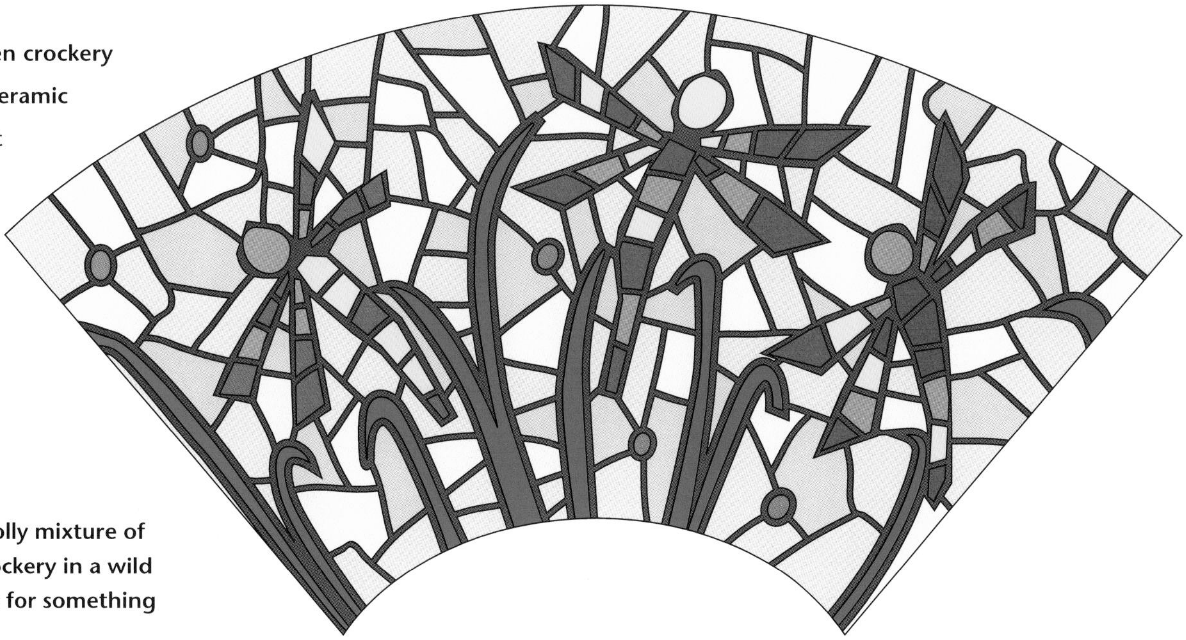

Or go for a bright, jolly mixture of ceramic tiles and crockery in a wild assortment of colors for something more funky.

Cool watery colors and overlapping waves provide a calm and soothing surround for this mirror and backsplash, based on a traditional Japanese repeating pattern. Although this particular project is made on a wooden backing board, it could be applied directly to the area above the sink.

Overlapping Wave Backsplash

Materials
tracing paper
pencil
marking pen
unglazed ceramic tesserae
white or yellow craft glue
gray grout
acrylic paint
particleboard
mirror
sandpaper

Equipment
jigsaw
mask and safety glasses
mosaic nippers
tile cutters
small trowel
paintbrush
squeegee
bucket
sponge
cloth

Modify and trace the design
Measure the width of the sink and area above for the backsplash and mirror. Enlarge and modify the design accordingly and trace the adapted design onto particleboard, clearly defining the outline with a marking pen.

Cut and prepare the wood
Using a jigsaw, carefully cut the wood along the outline. Smooth the rough edges away with sandpaper and prepare the surface of the wood with a solution of craft glue and water (1 part glue: 4 parts water). Do this on both sides of the wood to protect it from bathroom condensation and to avoid warping. Allow to dry thoroughly before doing the mosaic.

Glue the mirror
Measure the size of mirror you require and have this cut by a professional glass cutter. Stick the mirror into position on the wooden board with a generous layer of craft glue. Press down firmly and let dry.

Begin sticking down tesserae
Break the ceramic tiles into small squares using the tile cutters, which can be nibbled into shape later on, or use little ceramic mosaic tiles that do not require much in the way of cutting at this stage. Keep the ceramic tesserae in piles of the same color and give each color a number. Mark the numbers of the colors onto the board according to the design. Starting with the outside edge, begin sticking the tesserae into position with a small dab of craft glue, using each of the colors in turn. You may not want to be that systematic, but try not to get tesserae of the same color side by side around the edge. Once all the squares are in position around the edge, begin working on the inside section of the mosaic.

Complete sticking and allow to dry
Using the mosaic nippers, snip away at the corners of the ceramic squares to taper them into shape. Position the tesserae so they create an even flow around the curved shapes of the design. When all the tesserae have been affixed in place, let the project dry overnight before grouting.

Make powdered gray grout
In a bucket add water to powdered gray grout until it reaches a smooth buttery consistency. If you have only plain white grout this can be colored by adding grout dye or pigment to the water before mixing with the powder. Remember that the grout will usually dry much lighter, so it might be worth doing a sample first.

John Danson

Template

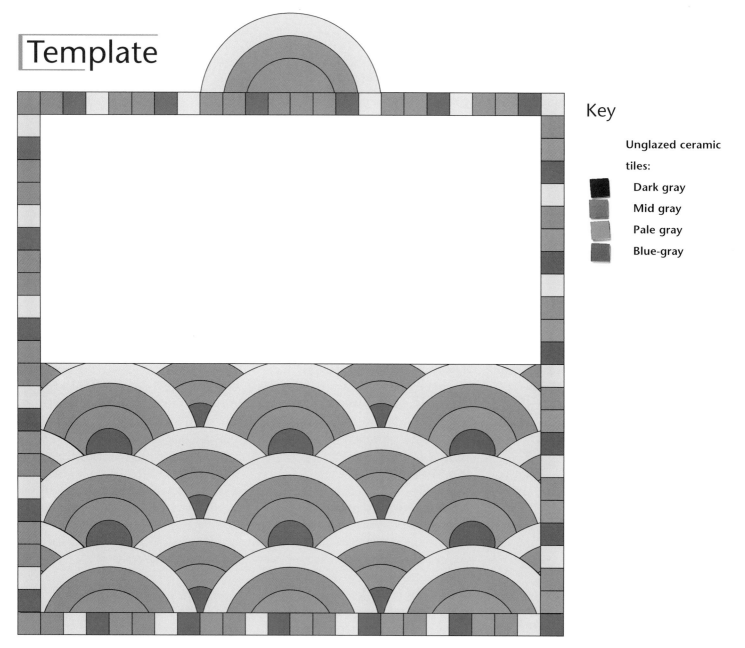

Key

Unglazed ceramic tiles:

Dark gray
Mid gray
Pale gray
Blue-gray

Grout the mosaic

Spread the grout over the mosaic with a small trowel, being careful not to scratch the mirror, and pushing the grout well into the spaces between the tesserae. Wipe off excess lumps with a rubber squeegee.

Wipe down and polish the mosaic

Take a damp sponge and wipe the surface of the mosaic to remove any remaining grout. When the grout is dry to the touch, polish it with a dry lint-free cloth.

TIP Rub any lumps of stray grout from the sides of the backsplash with sandpaper to make sure the surface is entirely smooth. Mix up acrylic paint to match the shade of grout used—in this case a pale gray. Carefully paint the edges of the wood with the acrylic paint and allow to dry thoroughly before attaching to the wall. Alternatively, you may want to use the same gloss paint as your bathroom woodwork. In this case you will need to use primer and then two coats of gloss paint.

Allow to dry and then affix to wall

Allow the mosaic to dry thoroughly, somewhere flat, for a couple of days before fixing it to the wall above the sink.

Color Options

Cool muted tones of unglazed ceramic tiles are just one option for this classic backsplash mirror. You could choose colors to complement your bathroom and incorporate any existing tiles that you may have spare.

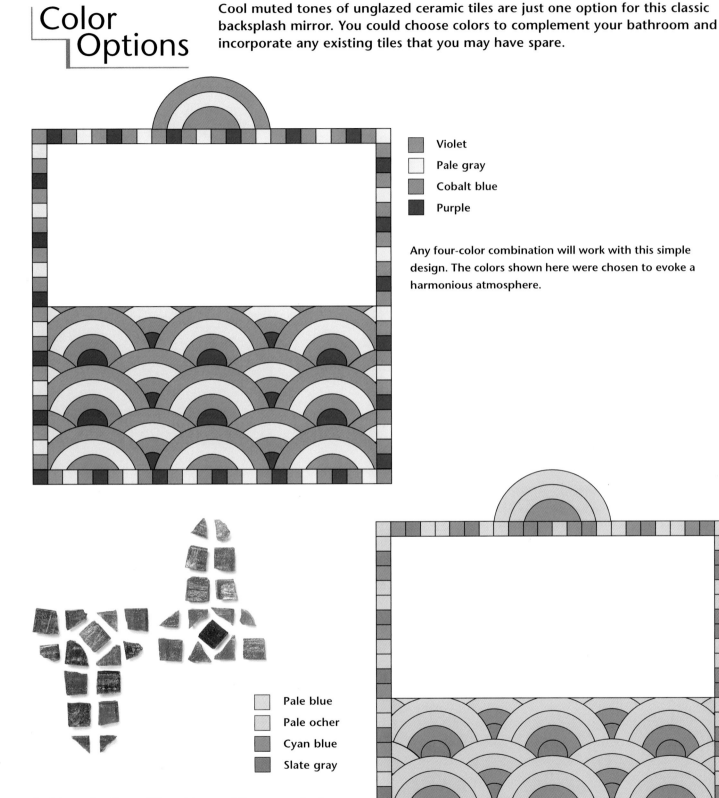

Violet

Pale gray

Cobalt blue

Purple

Any four-color combination will work with this simple design. The colors shown here were chosen to evoke a harmonious atmosphere.

Pale blue

Pale ocher

Cyan blue

Slate gray

In this version three different tones of the same color have been chosen, with the addition of one complementary color to bring in a bit of contrast.

At the turn of the century, with the advent of Art Nouveau, mosaics once again became popular—part of a renewed interest in all of the decorative arts. People began to explore different means of expression and, no longer needing to be representational, mosaics could be enjoyed for purely decorative purposes, allowing the introduction of abstract patterns and stylized forms.

MODERN INSPIRATIONS

Antoni Gaudí (1852–1926), perhaps the most outstanding of early twentieth century architects, pioneered the use of modern exterior mosaics. Covering vast expanses in broken ceramic, colored stones, glass, glazed tiles and marble, he achieved incredible effects, leading the way for three dimensional work and sculpture to be applied with mosaic. Parc Guell, in Barcelona, was transformed by Gaudí into one of his most fantastic creations, where colonnades, fountains, arcades, and a long undulating park bench, were covered in a dazzling array of colored ceramic tiles and broken plates. Rooftops and buildings around Barcelona were decorated in this way, reflecting light and sparkling in the sunshine.

Another prominent artist of this time who used mosaics was Gustav Klimt. His cartoon "Fulfilment" was later realized on the walls of the Palais Stoclet in Brussels—a long frieze of semi-precious stones, enamels and other luxurious materials. Many of Klimt's paintings have a mosaic feel about them, with their use of dazzling squares of color and the jewel-like colors of backgrounds set against highly decorative figures. Later, other fine artists such as Marc Chagall and Oskar Kokoshka turned their paintings into mosaic, although these were more of an exercise in using different materials than exploiting mosaic to its maximum potential.

"Fulfilment" by Gustave Klimt (1862–1918) was a preparatory work for the Stoclet freize. It uses mixed media and combines realistic segments with stylized patterns.

Antoni Gaudí used shapes inspired by natural forms, and covered curving surfaces in ceramic mosaic for the roof of the Gatehouse in Parc Guell, Barcelona.

Mosaic making all but disappeared during the war years and was later to reappear in rather dull architectural features during the fifties and sixties, during which time mosaics were used to decorate uninspiring pedestrian walkways and swimming pools. Mosaics didn't vanish completely however, and the spirit has been kept alive during the mid twentieth century by modern artists such as Niki de Saint Phalle (Il Giardino dei Tarocchi, in Tuscany), Raymon Eduoard Isidore (La Maison Picassiette, in Chartres) and Nek Chand (The Rock Garden, Chandigarh in India), whose imaginative mosaics use a variety of scrap, glass and china.

Now, with the mass production of tesserae and the readily available sources of more interesting materials, mosaicists have turned back to creating far more interesting and visually appealing works. Modern mosaicists are not bound by any one set of ideals—anything is possible, and mosaics no longer need to be representational, which gives the artist total freedom. Public works of art in mosaic are now a common sight; for example, the Underground station at Tottenham Court Road in London is extensively decorated with mosaics made using a variety of smalti, vitreous glass tesserae and ceramic, depicting designs of a musical and mechanical theme and cheering up thousands of weary commuters every day. Recently mosaics have seen something of a revival—no longer exclusively for the very wealthy, mosaics can be made and enjoyed by all people from all walks of life.

This lizard fountain is just one of Gaudí's many stunning mosaics set in the beautiful gardens of Parc Guell, Barcellona.

Belgian architect Victor Horta (1861–1947) used mosaic as an integral part of the whole design for his elegant Art Nouveau interiors, such as this floor at the Van Eetuelde House in Brussels.

Themes

figures, modern art, architecture, folk art

Designs

abstract patterns and shapes, bright colors

Materials

broken plates, glazed tiles, smalti, mirror, beads, bottle caps

Objects

furniture, jewelry, fountains, benches, fireplaces

Places

BARCELONA
Park Guell, Finca Guell, Casa Battlo, Casa Mila, Sagrada Familia— Antoni Gaudí

INDIA
The Rock Garden, Chandigarh—Nek Chand

NICE
Faculty of Law, Nice University—Marc Chagall

LONDON
Tottenham Court Road Underground station— Eduardo Paolozzi

NEW YORK
William O'Grady High School, Coney Island— Ben Shahn

These bright modern candlesticks are a great starter project. They are of a manageable size and you can use pieces of broken tiles, old china or just about anything else that you like or happen to have lying around. Add a few pieces of reflective or shiny tesserae and these candlesticks will look fantastic in dim light.

Golden Candlesticks

Materials

sections of circular wood pole or prefabricated candlesticks
white or yellow craft glue
multicolored ceramic tiles
tile adhesive
powdered white grout
gold paint

Equipment

sandpaper
mask and safety glasses
tile cutters
mosaic nippers
palette knife
bucket
sponge and cloths
paintbrushes

Prepare your candlesticks

First find a suitable candlestick base to work on—in this instance a base was specially designed and made by turning a section of wood on an electric lathe. You can work on any simple candlestick that has no unnecessary grooves, bumps or ridges on the column. Rub off any varnish or paint on the base with coarse sandpaper and apply a solution of craft glue and water (1 part glue: 4 parts water) with a paintbrush and allow to dry thoroughly.

Cut your tesserae

Break up a selection of ceramic tiles of varying colors and patterns. The pieces need to be fairly small as they have to fit around a curve, but don't worry about the shapes at this stage as they will need to be nibbled into exact shapes later on. Mix up all the tesserae into one big pile.

Stick the tesserae on

Select the tesserae at random from the pile, nibbling into shape as required. Apply a small dab of tile adhesive to the back of the tesserae before pressing them firmly onto the wood. Starting at the top and working down, work on one section of the candlestick at a time, so you always have a secure part to hold onto while you work. Once all the tesserae are in place let the candlestick dry overnight.

Grout the candlesticks

Mix up the grout in a bucket—white grout is ideal but it doesn't matter too much since the grout will be painted later. Apply the grout with a palette knife, pushing down in between the spaces and smoothing off any rough edges around the column. Wipe away any excess grout with a damp sponge and polish with a dry lint-free cloth when the grout is dry to the touch. Allow the candlestick to dry thoroughly for at least two days before the next stage.

Steve Wright and Donald Jones

Finish off with gold paint
Paint over the grout using a fine paint-brush and shiny gold paint (see Tip).

Template

TIP Add the finishing touches to this candlestick by painting the grout with a shiny gold paint. Apply the paint with a fine artist's paintbrush to the spaces in between the tesserae. It is quite a tricky job, but any stray drips of paint can be easily wiped off with a damp cloth. Allow the paint to dry thoroughly before using the candlesticks. Of course if your preference is for a different color scheme to suit your room, silver paint or any other metallic color would be equally effective.

Key

A mixture of multicolored pottery and patterned tiles

Bright gold-painted grout

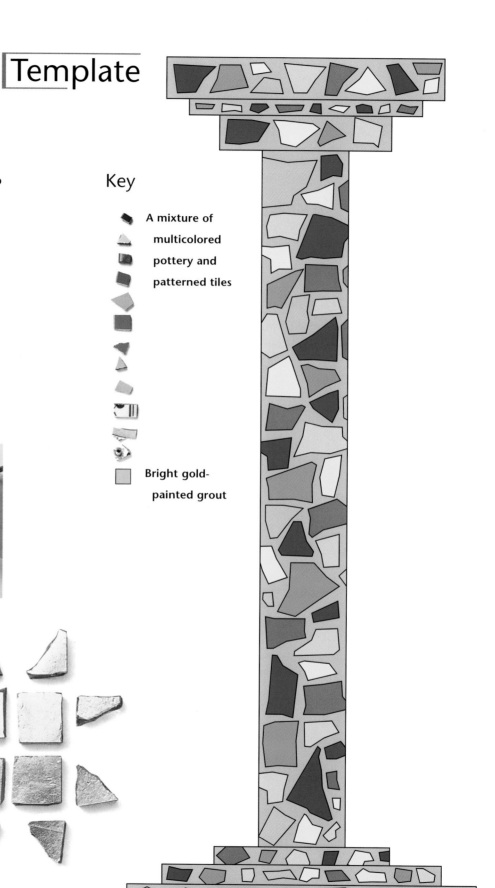

Color Options

Here's a chance to be truly experimental—there are no definite rules for this project as there is no particular pattern to follow, so either choose one of the color schemes shown or simply let your imagination run free.

Black patterned pottery with white grout
White patterned pottery with black grout

Ceramic tiles:

Pale turquoise
Light blue
Violet
White grout

This variation uses an assortment of bright, summery colors jumbled together then randomly spaced for a fresh modern flavor.

Alternating the color of the grout from black to white for each section up and down the column is a great way of achieving maximum contrast.

Blue
Flow Panel

Based on an original painting by the artist Susan Goldblatt, this mosaic draws the onlooker deep into the intricate flowing rhythms of the tesserae, evoking the sensations of movement and water.

Materials
particleboard
white or yellow craft glue
pencil and marking pen
strong brown wrapping paper
wallpaper paste
vitreous glass tesserae
cement based fixative
fine grout
supporting board

Equipment
mask and safety glasses
mosaic nippers
rubber gloves
bucket
paintbrush
sponge
notched trowel
flat trowel

Susan Goldblatt

Before you start
For this project you will need two boards. One is the backing board that the mosaic will be attached to and the other is to support the backing paper while you affix the tesserae. The supporting board should be a few inches larger than the mosaic backing board.

Prepare your base
Scratch the surface of the backing board with a sharp craft knife making a deep criss-cross pattern all over. This will help your adhesive to grip. Seal the surface by applying a solution of craft glue and water (1 part glue: 4 parts water) and allow to dry thoroughly.

Transfer your design
Lay brown paper over the supporting board with the shiny side facing upward. Remember that you are working indirectly, and that the outlines will be the reverse of the original design. It is useful to have two versions of the design, one of the original and one in the reverse to refer to when sticking the tesserae into place. Transfer the design onto the paper with a pencil, clearly marking the outlines and writing the colors in their appropriate places.

Stick the tesserae onto the paper
Use mosaic nippers to cut the tesserae to the exact sizes and stick the flat side of the tesserae onto the backing paper with

TIP To transfer the design onto the paper without tracing, draw up two grids. Draw the first grid over the template, breaking the design up into square sections. Then draw a larger grid with the same amount of squares onto the backing paper. Working on one square at a time, carefully copy the design from the template. This method creates a more personalized, freehand style rather than an exact replica of the template.

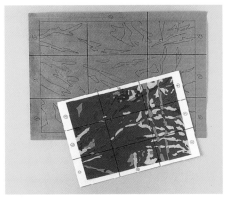

a small amount of wallpaper paste applied with a paintbrush. Mix up a strong solution of the paste but use it sparingly to avoid it seeping through the backing paper and sticking to the supporting board.

Space the tesserae evenly and carefully to create a sense of flow; work methodically

Template

using one color at a time, using the reverse version of the design for reference. In this project it is not necessary to divide the paper into sections—it can be worked on as one whole piece.

Transfer to the board

When all the tesserae are stuck into position, prepare the mosaic backing board with cement based fixative. Spread on with a notched trowel and make sure you have an even coverage. Flip the board over—you will need to get somebody to help you do this as the board becomes very heavy when covered in wet cement. Position the board right over the mosaic and press down hard

into place. Flip the boards over once again and remove the supporting board, so that you are left with just the mosaic on top of the backing board. Use a flat trowel to level the surface of the mosaic.

Finish with grout

Allow the mosaic to dry for three to four days before removing the paper. Wet the paper with a sponge and peel it back, keeping it close to the mosaic. Remove any stubborn paper by gently rubbing with the sponge. Grout the mosaic with a dark grout—using a dark color is important as it brings out the color of the tesserae.

Key

Vitreous glass:

Navy

Dark turquoise

Sea green

Green

Pale blue

Purple

Cobalt

Color Options

Choose tones and intensity of color to reflect the mood you wish to evoke. The two variations shown here demonstrate the dramatic differences in atmosphere created by different groups of colors.

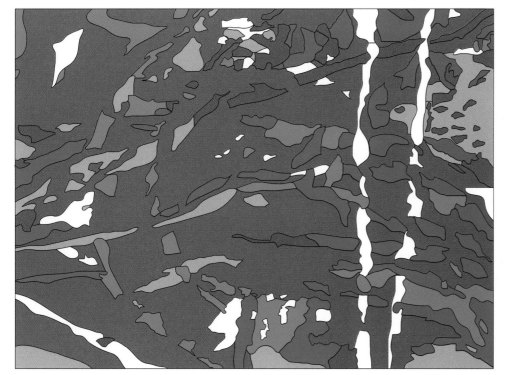

Ceramic tiles:

- White
- Fawn
- Dark terracotta
- Cyan blue
- Bright green
- Dark green

Dark, moody colors with ripples of white and bright green give a strong sense of movement and evoke the sensation of underlying currents.

Ceramic tiles:

- White
- Cream
- Sky blue
- Cobalt
- Leaf green
- Dark green

Soothing watery blues, dreamy white and soft cream . . . this version combines smooth tactile tesserae with tranquil colors to create a completely different mood.

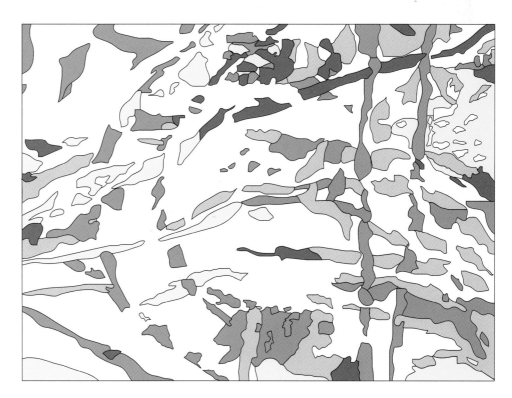

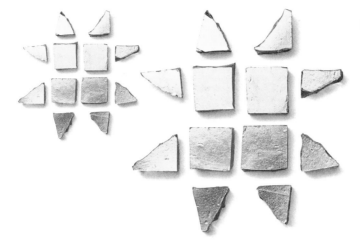

It is a big project, but a front door made from mosaic can be the crowning jewel of a beautiful home. It is also a great way of fixing up an old door that's looking a little worn out. This mirrored door gets a good deal of natural sunlight and fills the room with an amazing display of light.

Multicolored Door

Materials
mirror glass
ceramic tiles
broken china
tile adhesive
white grout
masking tape
gloss paint
white or yellow craft glue

Equipment
glass scorer and cutter
tile cutters
mosaic nippers
mask and safety glasses
trowel
bucket
squeegee
sponge and rags
paintbrush

TIP Prepare the surface of the door by sanding away any old paint or varnish. This can, of course, be done with sandpaper, but when working on large areas it is worth borrowing an electric sander. Cover nearby furniture with drop cloths, open the windows before you start and always wear a dust mask and protective glasses. Be careful when working around door handles and hinges; any grooves or hard to reach places can be finished off with sandpaper.

Clean the surface
Prepare the door by sanding down the gloss paint or varnish—you don't need to take it down to the bare wood, just take off the shiny surface. This is best done with an electric sander. Clean away dust and seal with a solution of water and craft glue (1 part glue: 4 parts water). Allow to dry thoroughly.

Decorate the panels
Starting on the middle panels first, break up a selection of colored and patterned ceramic tiles, broken china and white ceramic using the tile cutters and mosaic nippers. Put all the pieces in a pile together so they can be randomly selected. Nibble them into shape and stick them on the door with tile adhesive. Allow to dry while working on the rest of the mosaic.

Add the mirror sections
Break up sheets of mirror into manageable sizes before cutting down into smaller tesserae. Be extremely careful while cutting the mirror—wear a safety mask and glasses and work outdoors for this stage if possible. Stick the mirror tesserae on the

Steve Wright assisted by Marilyn Mansell

door with tile adhesive, starting from the outside edge and working toward the center, aligning flat edges of the pieces along the edges of the door, and using smaller tesserae to work around the door handle. Prop the door open so the mosaic cannot be disturbed and let it dry for a couple of days before grouting.

Grout the mosaic

Mix up white grout in a bucket and apply it to the mosaic with a trowel. Be gentle with the mirrored sections as the surface scratches fairly easily. Wipe off the excess with a rubber squeegee. Work in sections, starting with the ceramic mosaic panels and be careful not to spread grout into the wooden grooves—if this does happen, quickly wipe it away with a damp sponge. When the grout is dry to the touch, polish it with a dry cloth.

Paint the remaining areas

Let the grout set completely before painting the wooden inlays and door frame. Cover the mosaic with newspaper, securing the edges with masking tape. Paint the wood with gloss or semigloss, keeping the door securely propped open until the paint is completely dry.

Template

Key

Multicolored and
patterned pottery

Mirror glass

White ceramic

White grout

Yellow ocher painted
wood surround

Turquoise painted door
handle

Color
Options

The color scheme for a large project such as this rather depends on the setting, so you might wish to coordinate the colors to suit the room, or alternatively go wild and create something outrageous that will make a truly lasting impression.

The brighly painted wooden surround adds the finishing touch to this fantastic assortment of multicolored china and broken tiles.

- Mirror glass with white grout
- Blue and white willow pattern
-   pottery
- Ultramarine painted wood surround
- Black grout
- White gloss painted door handle

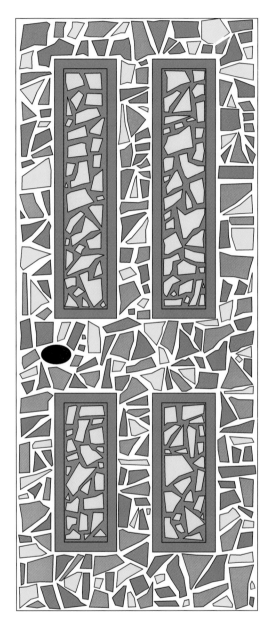

A dramatic result has been achieved here by using black grout against subtly patterned tiles. White grout against shards of mirror in the panels gives a great, contrasting look.

Ceramic tiles:
- Yellow
- Bright green
- Sky blue
- Bright pink
- Bright green painted wood surround
- Pale blue grout
- White grout
- Black gloss door handle

Standing inside this room is like being transported into a glittering world. Every surface of this dazzling bathroom is covered in hundreds and thousands of pieces of mirrored tesserae. Close the door behind you and reflections bounce off in all directions, shattering into a million pieces and stretching into eternity.

Glittery Mirror Bathroom

Materials
sheets of mirror
white or yellow craft glue
spackling compound
tile adhesive
grout

Equipment
glass cutters
mask and safety glasses
trowel
bucket
rubber gloves
squeegee
fine sandpaper
sponge and cloths
glass scraper

Prepare the surfaces

A project of this size requires a great deal of planning and time, especially if you intend to cover every available surface in mosaic. The walls, ceiling and other surfaces must be stable enough to handle the weight of the mosaic. Make sure that the surfaces are clean and dust-free and any existing problems with damp have been rectified before preparing with a craft glue and water solution (1 part glue: 1 part water). In this particular case, professional builders prepared the walls and ceiling by installing particleboard paneling ready to work on.

Cut your mirror tesserae

Draw up a plan of the room and measure out the surface area where the mosaic will go, to calculate how much mirror will be needed. Cut up plenty of mirror tesserae into several buckets, each containing different shapes and sizes. Cutting mirror requires great care—see Tip.

|TIP Find a space outdoors or somewhere very well ventilated to cut the mirror tesserae. Wearing a mask and safety glasses, cut the sheets of mirror into manageable sizes before breaking down into small tesserae. Glass shards are extremely hazardous, often barely visible, and have a tendency to fly off at obscure angles. Wear heavy-duty rubber gloves when cutting mirror and take extra care when laying the tesserae to avoid cutting your hands.

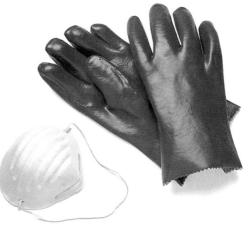

Start with the ceiling

Start with the ceiling, working in the direct method and beginning along one edge. It is a good idea to get somebody to help you at this stage, especially if you are balancing on a ladder. Make sure the mirror tesserae are securely attached to the ceiling using tile adhesive. Position larger pieces of mirror and then fill in the spaces with smaller ones, being careful with the edges around the light fixtures or extractor fans. Allow to dry thoroughly before

Fran Soler

Template

Key

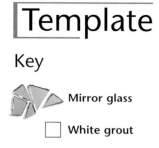

Mirror glass

White grout

The template here is intended as a guide rather than an exact format. If working with colored ceramic tiles, try to get a balance between colors and small and large pieces, and space the very bright tones evenly around the surfaces.

grouting—work on other areas and come back to it later. Working on ceilings is very time consuming and physically demanding—particularly on the arms and neck—so allow plenty of time for this stage.

Continue with the walls

When working on the walls, begin at the top and go all the way along and then work downward. Make sure all the surfaces are smooth to the touch and there are no sharp edges anywhere. You may want to install a "whole" mirror somewhere on the wall, such as above the sink or next to the shower—it is best to do this before you begin putting in the mosaic. Any bathroom fixtures, such as towel rails or shelving, should also be installed beforehand.

Complete the door

Sand away paint or varnish from the door and fill cracks with spackling compound, so that the surface of the door is as flat as possible. Prepare the door with a glue and water solution as before. Be extremely careful when laying the tesserae to make sure that the door still opens and closes easily.

Grout the room

For very large projects use a standard color powdered grout, otherwise you may run into problems mixing up multiple batches of grout that are the exact same color. Begin grouting the first area of the room where you put the mosaic and work around the room in the same order as before—this will guarantee that all the tile adhesive has had plenty of time to set. Apply grout

gently to the mosaic with a trowel, as mirror scratches very easily. Wipe away the excess grout with a rubber squeegee: after a while you may find that the sharp edges of the mirror begin to shred the rubber, leaving little bits on the tesserae. Wipe any away with a damp sponge and polish with a lint-free cloth once the surface is dry to the touch.

Smooth any sharp edges

Grouting needs to be done very thoroughly, to make a smooth surface throughout the room. Make sure that all corners are completely smooth and safe—if there are any sharp edges, gently rub down with fine sandpaper. Do not use mirror for a mosaic on the floor as glass is not strong or durable enough to be walked on.

Color Options

You can be as outrageous as you want in the privacy of your own bathroom, so choose colors to suit the mood you wish to create—warm reds and hot pinks or cool blues and icy whites. Whatever you fancy—anything goes!

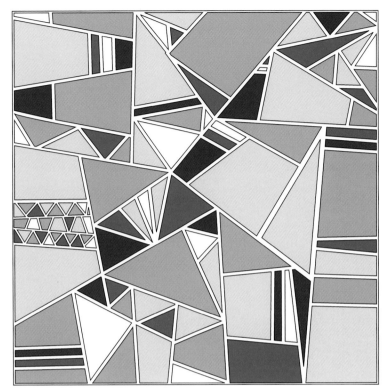

Ceramic tiles:

- Pale ocher
- Terracotta
- Orange
- Bright pink
- Cobalt blue
- Dark terracotta grout

A combination of different blues and shades of sea-green, with no mirror tiles at all, would give a cool, watery feel to the whole room.

Ceramic tiles:

- White
- Sky blue
- Turquoise
- Cobalt blue
- Navy
- White grout

At the other end of the spectrum, this option has a combination of strong colors in bright hues to give a warm and inviting atmosphere.

Inspired by the rich colors and complex swirling patterns of paintings by early twentieth century artists such as Klimt and Toulouse-Lautrec, this design brings to life an otherwise ordinary picture frame. Designs such as these need not be confined to mundane objects—at the turn of the century, with the advent of Art Nouveau, almost anything that could be decorated usually was.

Art Nouveau
Picture Frame

Materials
picture frame
spackling compound
sandpaper
marking pen
white or yellow craft glue
gold smalti
vitreous glass tesserae
toothpicks
grout
gold paint

Equipment
mask and safety glasses
tile cutters
mosaic nippers
paintbrush
squeegee
palette knife
bucket
sponge
dry cloth

Prepare the picture frame

When choosing a picture frame for your base, try to find one that has a simple, plain surface. Remove the glass and backing from the frame and keep them somewhere safe. Use coarse sandpaper to rough up the surface or take away unwanted varnish and apply a layer of craft glue and water (1 part glue: 4 parts water) with a paintbrush and allow to dry thoroughly. If your picture frame has grooves or an inlaid pattern, fill in the holes with spackling compound and smooth it with a squeegee so that the surface is completely flat. When the spackling compound has dried, apply another layer of glue and water solution and allow it to dry once again.

Transfer the design onto the frame

Modify the design to fit the size and shape of your frame. Trace the design onto the frame and define the outlines with a marking pen. Simplify the design if you are working on a very small frame as the smaller the design, the more tricky and complicated it will become.

Make the gold swirls

Use gold smalti for the swirl details, using mosaic nippers to cut them into the exact shape and size, and stick them in place with a small amount of craft glue. Use a toothpick or any fine-pointed tool to help create even spaces between the tesserae. Complete all the gold swirls before filling in the background with colored tesserae.

Fran Soler

Template

Key

Vitreous glass:

- Blue
- Pale pink
- Fawn
- Gold-veined blue
- Pale green
- Sea green
- Gold-veined green
- Pale fawn
- Pale gray
- Brown
- Pink
- Charcoal
- Gold smalti
- Gold-painted grout

Grout and smooth the mosaic

When all the tesserae are in place, let the picture frame dry before grouting with a fine white grout. Carefully spread the grout over the mosaic with a palette knife and smooth it with a squeegee, making sure that the edges are smooth. Wipe a damp cloth over the surface to remove any remaining grout and let rest until touch dry before polishing with a dry lint-free cloth.

Apply gold paint and reassemble

Allow to dry for a couple of days before painting the grout and the edge of the frame with gold paint. Make sure the paint has completely dried before affixing the glass and backing to the frame.

TIP When working with very small tesserae it can be extremely frustrating trying to get the pieces into exact position. Toothpicks (or any other fine pointed instrument) can be used to gently nudge the tesserae into place and are invaluable for delicate work, particularly to even-out the gaps between tesserae.

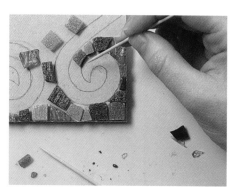

Color Options

Contrasting swirls of twinkling tesserae against a mellow background or a concoction of coordinating colors? Select the tesserae you desire to enhance your favorite picture.

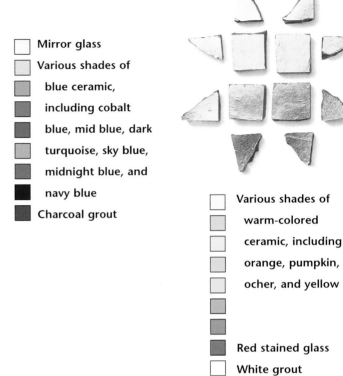

- Mirror glass
- Various shades of
- blue ceramic,
- including cobalt
- blue, mid blue, dark
- turquoise, sky blue,
- midnight blue, and
- navy blue
- Charcoal grout

This eye-catching variation has sparkling swirls of mirror against a brilliant blue background for a totally different look.

- Various shades of
- warm-colored
- ceramic, including
- orange, pumpkin,
- ocher, and yellow
- Red stained glass
- White grout

Create a bold statement with shimmering stained glass swirls and a cheerful mixture of bright oranges and yellows in shiny ceramic for the background.

Index

Color Options

Contrasting swirls of twinkling tesserae against a mellow background or a concoction of coordinating colors? Select the tesserae you desire to enhance your favorite picture.

- ☐ Mirror glass
- ☐ Various shades of
- blue ceramic,
- including cobalt
- blue, mid blue, dark
- turquoise, sky blue,
- midnight blue, and
- navy blue
- Charcoal grout

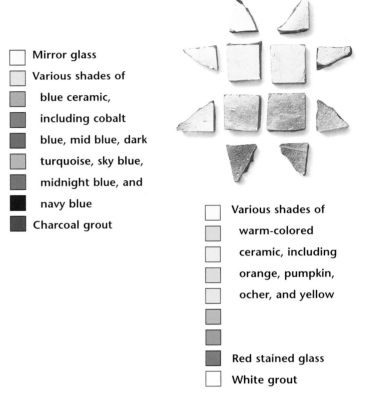

- ☐ Various shades of
- warm-colored
- ceramic, including
- orange, pumpkin,
- ocher, and yellow
- Red stained glass
- ☐ White grout

This eye-catching variation has sparkling swirls of mirror against a brilliant blue background for a totally different look.

Create a bold statement with shimmering stained glass swirls and a cheerful mixture of bright oranges and yellows in shiny ceramic for the background.

Index

Credits

Mosaic Credits

Quarto Publishing would like to thank the mosaic-makers who contributed projects for this book:

John Danson
Claire Foss
Susan Goldblatt
Katy Hall
Richard Hanson
Donald Jones
Tipper Lewis
Marilyn Mansell
Norma Vondee
Steve Wright

and particularly the author, Fran Soler, for her help in project-making, demonstrating techniques and coordinating the book.

The smalti and tesserae on pages 23 to 25 were supplied by courtesy of

The Mosaics Workshop, Unit B
443–449 Holloway Road
London
GB-N7 6LJ

The hammer and hardie on page 26 was supplied by courtesy of

Les Clifton
117 Highland Road,
Bromley, Kent
GB-BR1 4AA

Photographic Credits

Quarto Publishing would like to thank and acknowledge the following for providing pictures used on the following pages in this book:

AKG London: 61tl, 7tl, 36t & b, 87b, 104-5c, 105b
The British Museum, London: 55c
Clark/Clinch: 18c, 105tr
e. t. archive: 86tr, 87t
Pictor Uniphoto: 54b
Visual Arts Library: 6r, 7r, 37t, 54t, 55t, 72t & b, 73t

t = top, c = center, b = bottom,
l = left, r = right

All other photographs are the copyright of Quarto Publishing plc